CAMBRIDGE
Primary Science

Learner's Book 1

Jon Board & Alan Cross

CAMBRIDGE
UNIVERSITY PRESS

University Printing House, Cambridge CB2 8BS, United Kingdom

One Liberty Plaza, 20th Floor, New York, NY 10006, USA

477 Williamstown Road, Port Melbourne, VIC 3207, Australia

314–321, 3rd Floor, Plot 3, Splendor Forum, Jasola District Centre,
New Delhi – 110025, India

103 Penang Road, #05-06/07, Visioncrest Commercial, Singapore 238467

Cambridge University Press is part of the University of Cambridge.

It furthers the University's mission by disseminating knowledge in the pursuit of education, learning and research at the highest international levels of excellence.

www.cambridge.org
Information on this title: www.cambridge.org/9781108742726

© Cambridge University Press 2021

This publication is in copyright. Subject to statutory exception
and to the provisions of relevant collective licensing agreements,
no reproduction of any part may take place without the written
permission of Cambridge University Press.

First published 2014
Second edition 2021

20 19 18 17 16 15 14 13 12 11 10 9 8 7 6 5 4

Printed in Dubai by Oriental Press

A catalogue record for this publication is available from the British Library

ISBN 978-1-108-74272-6 Paperback with Digital Access (1 Year)
ISBN 978-1-108-97254-3 Digital Learner's Book (1 Year)
ISBN 978-1-108-97253-6 eBook

Additional resources for this publication at www.cambridge.org/delange

Cambridge University Press has no responsibility for the persistence or accuracy of URLs for external or third-party internet websites referred to in this publication, and does not guarantee that any content on such websites is, or will remain, accurate or appropriate. Information regarding prices, travel timetables, and other factual information given in this work is correct at the time of first printing but Cambridge University Press does not guarantee the accuracy of such information thereafter.

Cambridge International copyright material in this publication is reproduced under licence and remains the intellectual property of Cambridge Assessment International Education.

Third-party websites and resources referred to in this publication have not been endorsed by Cambridge Assessment International Education

NOTICE TO TEACHERS IN THE UK
It is illegal to reproduce any part of this work in material form (including photocopying and electronic storage) except under the following circumstances:
(i) where you are abiding by a licence granted to your school or institution by the Copyright Licensing Agency;
(ii) where no such licence exists, or where you wish to exceed the terms of a licence, and you have gained the written permission of Cambridge University Press;
(iii) where you are allowed to reproduce without permission under the provisions of Chapter 3 of the Copyright, Designs and Patents Act 1988, which covers, for example, the reproduction of short passages within certain types of educational anthology and reproduction for the purposes of setting examination questions.

Introduction

Welcome to Stage 1 of **Cambridge Primary Science**. We hope you will enjoy it. We know you will find the science topics interesting and the activities fun.

You are going to learn about:

- humans
- plants
- materials
- forces
- sound
- planet Earth.

We know that Stage 1 learners love to learn science and learn about the world. We will be asking you to talk about what you know already.

We know you can do science yourself, so each unit has lots of practical activities and investigations for you to try. You will need to ask questions and talk about ways to find out the answers. You will need to look at things carefully, talk and think about what you see and what you are learning. Don't be afraid of being wrong. This is an important part of learning new things. Scientists often get things wrong at first but then they find the answer!

There are also some projects where you can find out how science is used in the world around you and how the ideas of scientists have changed over time.

We hope you enjoy thinking and working like a scientist!

Jon Board and Alan Cross

Contents

Page	Unit	Science strand	Thinking and Working Scientifically strand	Science in Context
2 2 5 9 12	**1 Living things** 1.1 Animals and plants alive! 1.2 Parts of a plant 1.3 Plants and light 1.4 Plants need water	Biology: Structure and function Biology: Life processes	Scientific enquiry: purpose and planning Carrying out scientific enquiry Scientific enquiry: analysis, evaluation and conclusions	Know that everyone uses science and identify people who use science professionally.
20 20 26 32	**2 Sound** 2.1 Sound sources 2.2 Loud and quiet 2.3 Sound moves	Physics: Light and sound	Scientific enquiry: purpose and planning Carrying out scientific enquiry Scientific enquiry: analysis, evaluation and conclusions	Talk about how science explains how objects they use, or know about, work.
41 41 44 48 53	**3 Materials in my world** 3.1 Different materials 3.2 Properties of materials 3.3 Sorting materials 3.4 Changing materials	Chemistry: Materials and their structure Chemistry: Properties of materials Chemistry: Changes to materials	Scientific enquiry: purpose and planning Carrying out scientific enquiry Scientific enquiry: analysis, evaluation and conclusions	Talk about how science helps us understand our effect on the world around us.

Contents

Page	Unit	Science strand	Thinking and Working Scientifically strand	Science in Context
61 61 66 73 79	**4 The Earth** 4.1 Planet Earth 4.2 Heat and light from the Sun 4.3 Rocks 4.4 Soil	Earth and Space: Planet Earth Earth and Space: Earth in space	Scientific enquiry: purpose and planning Carrying out scientific enquiry	Talk about how science explains how objects they use, or know about, work.
88 88 92 96 99	**5 Humans** 5.1 Our bodies 5.2 Our amazing senses 5.3 Similar and different 5.4 Staying alive	Biology: Structure and function Biology: Life processes	Scientific enquiry: purpose and planning Carrying out scientific enquiry Scientific enquiry: analysis, evaluation and conclusions	Know that everyone uses science and identify people who use science professionally.
108 108 115 121 128 133	**6 Forces** 6.1 Moving things 6.2 Push and pull forces 6.3 Making things move 6.4 Floating and sinking 6.5 Magnets can pull	Physics: Forces and energy Physics: Electricity and magnetism	Scientific enquiry: purpose and planning Carrying out scientific enquiry Scientific enquiry: analysis, evaluation and conclusions	Talk about how science explains how objects they use, or know about, work.
141 145	**New science skills** **Glossary and Index**			

How to use this book

How to use this book

In this book you will find lots of different features to help your learning.

What you will learn in the topic.

We are going to:
- find living things and things that have never been alive
- draw some living things
- put things into groups.

Questions to find out what you know already.

Getting started
- Name some living things.
- Look around your classroom. Point to some things that are not alive.

Important words to learn.

answer   investigation
asks   light
grow   question

A fun activity about the science you are learning.

Activity

Healthy plants?
What could we do to help these plants grow?
What do you think will happen to these plants?
Tell other people what you predict.

A

B

If plants do not have enough water they can die.

If plants have too much water they can die.

An investigation to carry out with a partner or in groups.

Think like a scientist 1

How plants get water

Do plants get water through their leaves or roots?

Let's do a test!

You will need:
two plants, a plastic bag, string, a watering can

Zara pours water onto the leaves of one plant. She puts a plastic bag around the leaves of the other plant and waters the roots.

Predict what will happen.
Now try this science investigation.
Observe what happens.
Draw the plants before and after the investigation.

Make sure you wash your hands after touching the plants.

How to use this book

Questions to help you think about how you learn.

How did the hands-on work help you to learn today?

Look what I can do!
- ☐ I can explain why plants need water.
- ☐ I can record observations in tables.
- ☐ I can predict what will happen in a science investigation.
- ☐ I can say if what happened was what I predicted.

This is what you have learnt in the topic.

Check your progress

Talk about these questions.

1 Which pictures show a sound source?

Questions that cover what you have learnt in the unit. If you can answer these, you are ready to move on to the next unit.

Project

Gardens and gardeners

We all love to play in a garden.
In a garden we can learn about plants and how to care for them.

At the end of each unit, there is a project for you to do, using what you have learnt. You might make something or solve a problem.

Part 1
Draw a garden for school, home or the park.

1 Living things

1.1 Animals and plants alive!

We are going to:
- find living things and things that have never been alive
- draw some living things
- put things into groups.

alive look
animal non-living
group plant
living water

Getting started
- Name some living things.
- Look around your classroom. Point to some things that are not alive.

1.1 Animals and plants alive!

Use your eyes to **look** at the picture. What can you see?

Point to a **plant**. Most plants are green.

Plants make their own food.

Point to an **animal** in the picture.

Animals move around and eat other things.

Plants and animals are **alive**.

They are **living** things.

All living things need food.

Water moves but it is not alive.
Point to what is **non-living** in the picture.

Think like a scientist

What living things can we find?

You will need:
paper, a pencil, a clipboard or thick card to rest on, a digital camera

Go outside to look for living things.

Be careful in case there are plants or animals that are prickly, sting or bite.

Try to find four living things.

Draw and photograph some living things.

What is the largest living thing you can find?

What is the smallest living thing you can find?

3

1 Living things

Activity

Living or non-living?

Zara is putting things into two **groups**.

Where should she put the toy?

What other things could she put in the groups?

Look at the non-living things.

Point to something that used to be alive.

Point to some things that have never been alive.

Make a group of living things and a group of non-living things.

Use things from your classroom.

How do you know which things are alive?

How am I doing?

Ask a friend to look at your groups.
Have you put things in the right group?

How does putting things into groups help you learn science?

Look what I can do!

- ☐ I can name four or more things that are living.
- ☐ I can name four or more things that have never been alive.
- ☐ I can draw some living things.
- ☐ I can put things into two groups.

> 1.2 Parts of a plant

We are going to:
- find out about the parts of plants
- name the parts of plants
- draw parts of a plant.

Getting started

You know that plants are living.
- What parts of plants have you seen?
- Tell a friend about some parts of plants.

Plants are all around us.
Some plants are tall and some are small.
All plants have **parts** that we can see.
Some plants have flowers which make **seeds**.
We are going to learn about these plants and their parts.

different   observe
flower   parts
leaf   root
magnifying seeds
  glass   similar
model   stem
name

1 Living things

Activity 1

Finding plant parts

Plants have many parts.

Look carefully at the plant in the drawing.

What do you see or *observe*?

Point to a *leaf*, a *flower*, the *stem* and the *roots*.

Activity 2

Making a model plant

Sofia can tell us what the parts do.

Make a *model* of a plant with these parts.

Say what each part is for.

> The flower is the part where the seeds are made.

> The leaf makes food for the plant.

> The roots collect water. The roots hold the plant still.

> The stem holds the leaves and flowers up.

1.2 Parts of a plant

Think like a scientist

Observing plant parts

You will need:
a plant, a magnifying glass, paper, a pencil

Observe a plant.

Look carefully at the plant parts.

Do not eat plants you find and wash your hands after touching any plants.

Name the plant parts.

Observe three different plants.

Look at the plant parts.

Draw them.

Do they all look the same?

Are they similar or different?

How am I doing?

Play 'What am I?' with a friend.

Use the words leaf, stem, flower, root.

Say what each is for.

1 Living things

Do you find it easy to observe living things?
How does observing help you learn?

Look what I can do!
- ☐ I can find out about plants.
- ☐ I can name parts of a plant.
- ☐ I can draw parts of a plant.

> 1.3 Plants and light

We are going to:
- **find out if plants need light**
- **do an investigation and say what we think will happen.**

Getting started
- Where do you see plants?
- Do you have plants at home? Tell a friend where you keep plants at home.

answer　　investigation
asks　　　light
grow　　　question

Here are some young plants.

When plants get bigger we say they grow.

Activity

What do plants need to grow?

What do you think plants need to grow?

Talk with a friend. What do they think plants need?

Do plants need food and water like people?

Write or draw what you think plants need.

1 Living things

Marcus **asks** a **question**: 'Why is this plant bent?'

Here is the **answer**: 'It is growing towards the **light**.'

Think like a scientist

What happens to a plant with no light?

> **You will need:**
> two plants, a box

Marcus wants to answer this question. 'What will happen to a plant with no light?'

He covers one plant with a box.

He puts the other plant in the light.

Say or draw what you think will happen.

Try this **investigation** yourself to find out the answer.

How am I doing?

What places would be too dark for plants to grow?
Talk about your ideas or draw them.

1.3 Plants and light

Look at this cave.

Why are no plants growing inside?

Plants use light to make food.

Plants can't grow in the cave because there is no light.

> **Look what I can do!**
> ☐ I can say what will happen to a plant with no light.
> ☐ I can say what I think will happen in an investigation.

1 Living things

> 1.4 Plants need water

We are going to:
- learn about how plants need water
- record observations in tables
- predict what will happen in an investigation
- see if what happened was what we predicted.

Getting started
- Draw two things you know about plants.
- Show a friend what you have drawn.

explain   record
practical   table
predict

What should the children do to keep this plant alive?

Look at the leaves!

This plant needs water!

You may have seen plants growing in places like this.

Some plants live near water.

Some plants live in water.

Some plants live in dry places.

Where do plants get water from?

1.4 Plants need water

Activity

Healthy plants?

What could we do to help these plants grow?

What do you think will happen to these plants?

Tell other people what you **predict**.

A

B

If plants do not have enough water they can die.

If plants have too much water they can die.

Think like a scientist 1

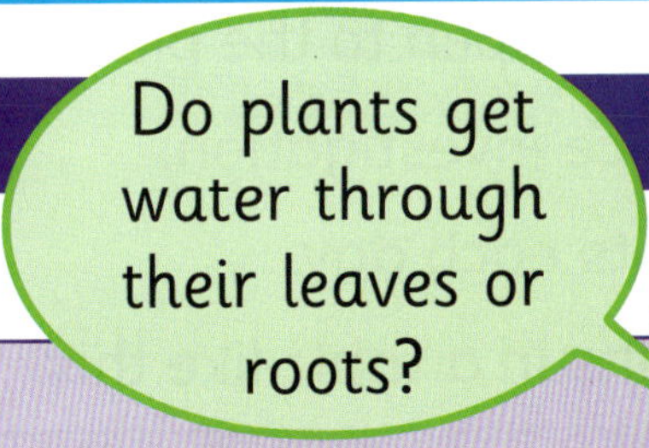

How plants get water

You will need:
two plants, a plastic bag, string, a watering can

Do plants get water through their leaves or roots?

Let's do a test!

Zara pours water onto the leaves of one plant. She puts a plastic bag around the leaves of the other plant and waters the roots.

Predict what will happen.
Now try this science investigation.
Observe what happens.
Draw the plants before and after the investigation.

Make sure you wash your hands after touching the plants.

13

1 Living things

Think like a scientist 2

How much water do plants need?

You will need: some plants, a watering can

Give some plants lots of water.

Give some plants a little water.

Give some plants no water.

Predict what will happen to the plants.

Now do the science investigation.

Observe the plants each day.

Record your results in a **table** like this.

How much water do the plants need? My table of results.			
	Water every day	Water two times each week	Do not water
Day 1			
Day 2			
Day 3			
Day 4			
Day 5			

Draw the plants in the table.

1.4 Plants need water

Continued

How am I doing?

Read what Lucas says.
What would you say to him?
Explain to Lucas why he is wrong.

Some plants do not need water.

How did the **practical** work help you to learn?

Look what I can do!

- ☐ I can explain why plants need water.
- ☐ I can record observations in tables.
- ☐ I can predict what will happen in a science investigation.
- ☐ I can say if what happened was what I predicted.

1 Living things

Project

Gardens and gardeners

We all love to play in a garden.

In a garden we can learn about plants and how to care for them.

Part 1

Draw a garden for school, home or the park.

Draw lots of different plants.

Who will look after the garden?

Draw the gardener.

What does the gardener do?

The gardener will give the plants lots of light and water.

Project

Continued

Part 2

Make a tiny garden in a tray or box.

Use your science to help you plan and make a garden.

These are some things you may need.

17

1 Living things

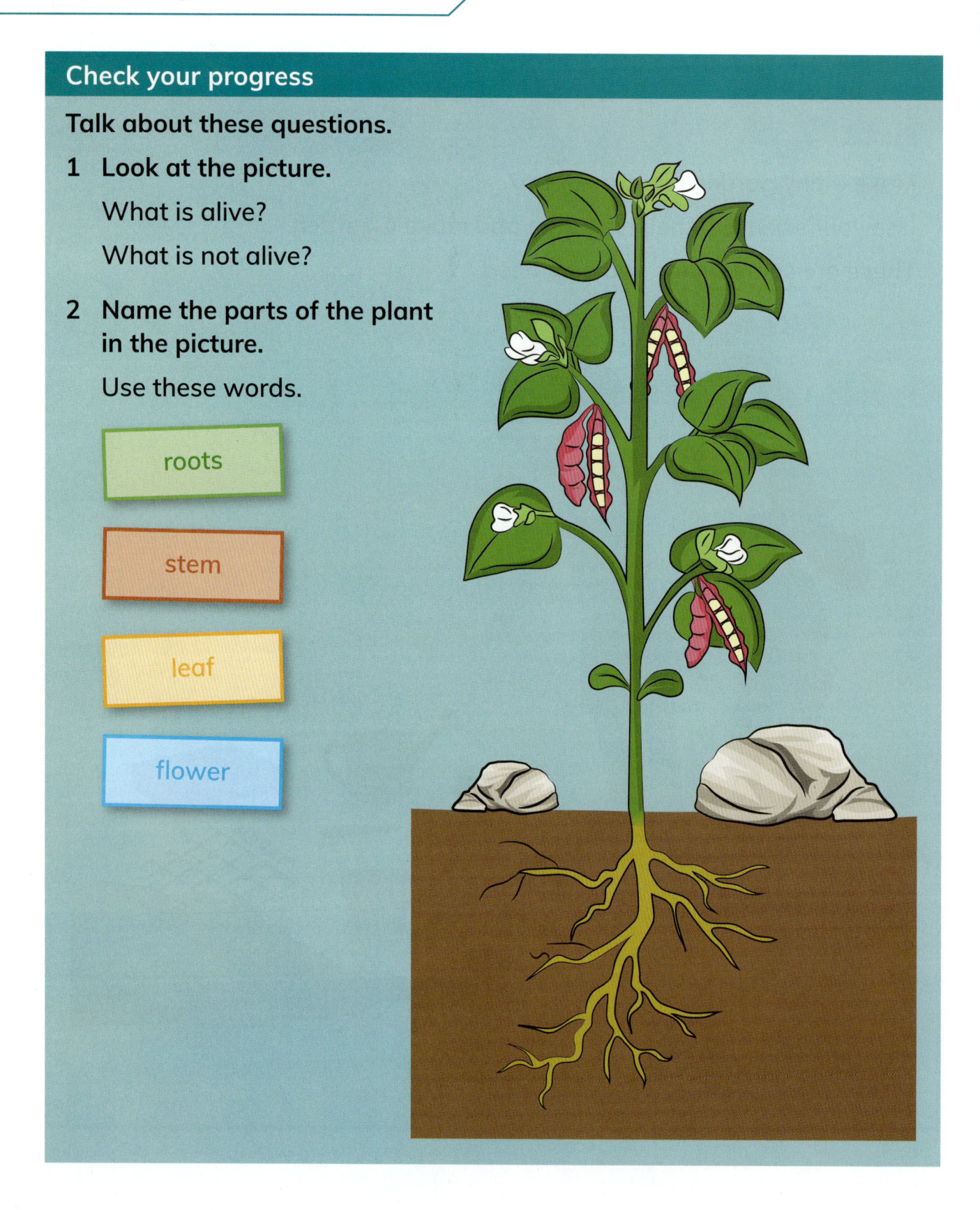

Check your progress

Talk about these questions.

1. Look at the picture.

   What is alive?

   What is not alive?

2. Name the parts of the plant in the picture.

   Use these words.

   roots

   stem

   leaf

   flower

Continued

3 What do these plants need?

4 Help Amy.

What do the seeds need to grow?

2 Sound

> 2.1 Sound sources

We are going to:

- find sources of sound
- say which sound sources use electricity
- make predictions and see if they are right
- collect and record observations.

Getting started

- Tell a friend about something you know that makes a sound.
- Listen then point to something that makes a sound.

ears   results
electricity   scientists
hear   sound
list   source

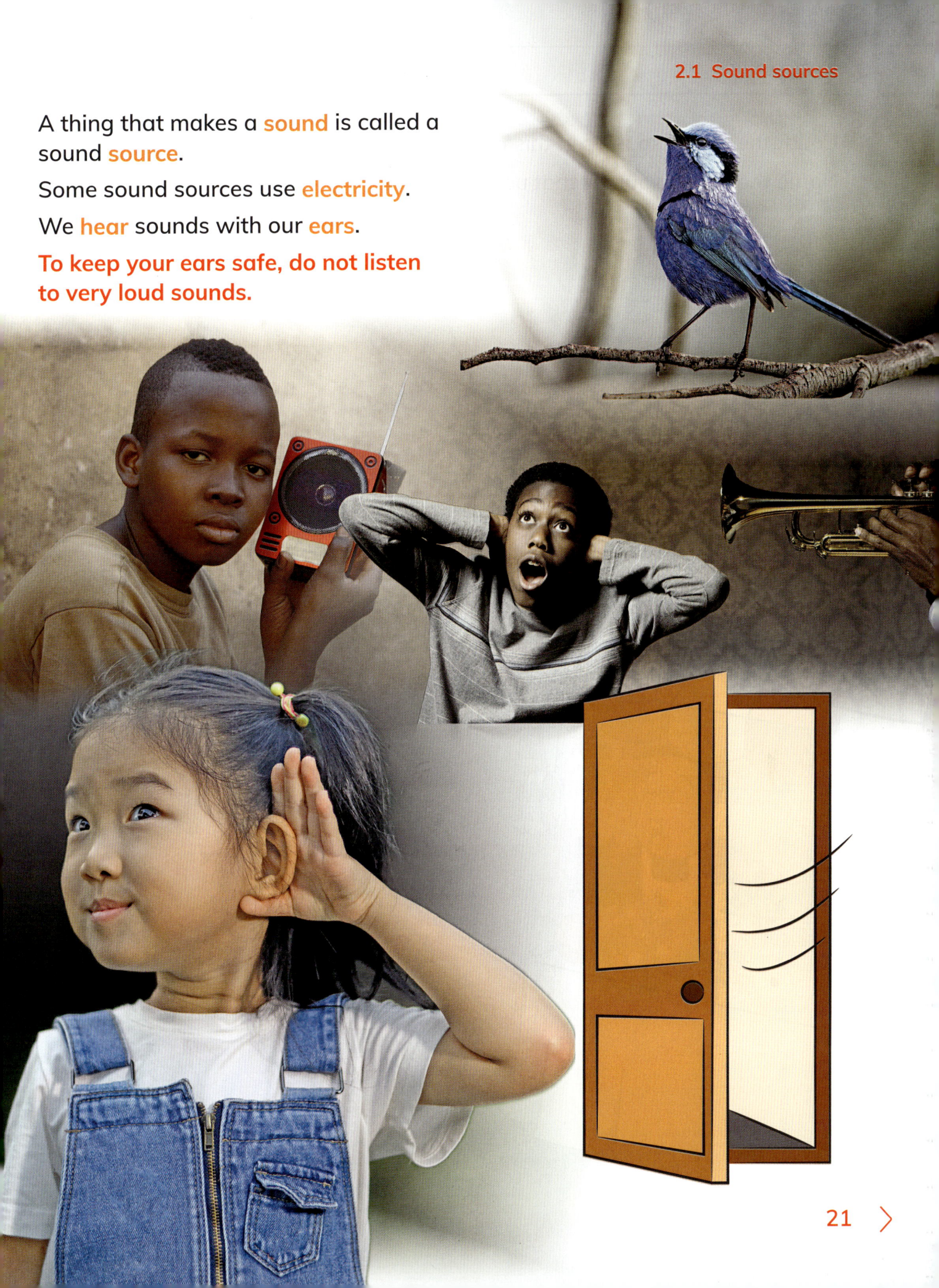

2.1 Sound sources

A thing that makes a **sound** is called a sound **source**.

Some sound sources use **electricity**.

We **hear** sounds with our **ears**.

To keep your ears safe, do not listen to very loud sounds.

21

2 Sound

Count the sound sources in this picture.

Name the sound sources that use electricity.

22

2.1 Sound sources

Activity

Sound sources in school

Walk around your school or classroom.

What sound sources will you find?

Before the walk, make a list like this.

> I predict that I will find …
>
> a clock

After your walk, what did you find?

Make a list like this:

> On our walk we found…
>
> a telephone

Did you find the things you predicted?

Which of the sound sources use electricity?

2 Sound

Think like a scientist

Find that sound!

> **You will need:**
> some sound sources,
> a blindfold

Scientists are people who do investigations to answer questions.

What you find out is called your **results**.

We will try to answer this question:

'**Can a friend point to sounds you make?**'

The children are investigating to see if Zara can point to the sound.

Talk to your friends about doing this investigation.

Plan which sound sources you will use.

Predict which things they can point to.

Write your prediction and results like this.

Can a friend point to these sounds?		
sound source	prediction	results
clock	yes 🙂	yes 🙂

2.1 Sound sources

> **Continued**
>
> Do the investigation with your friends.
>
> Which sounds were easy to find?
>
> **How am I doing?**
>
> Were some of your predictions wrong?
>
> When predictions are wrong it shows we have learnt something new.

How do investigations help you learn science?

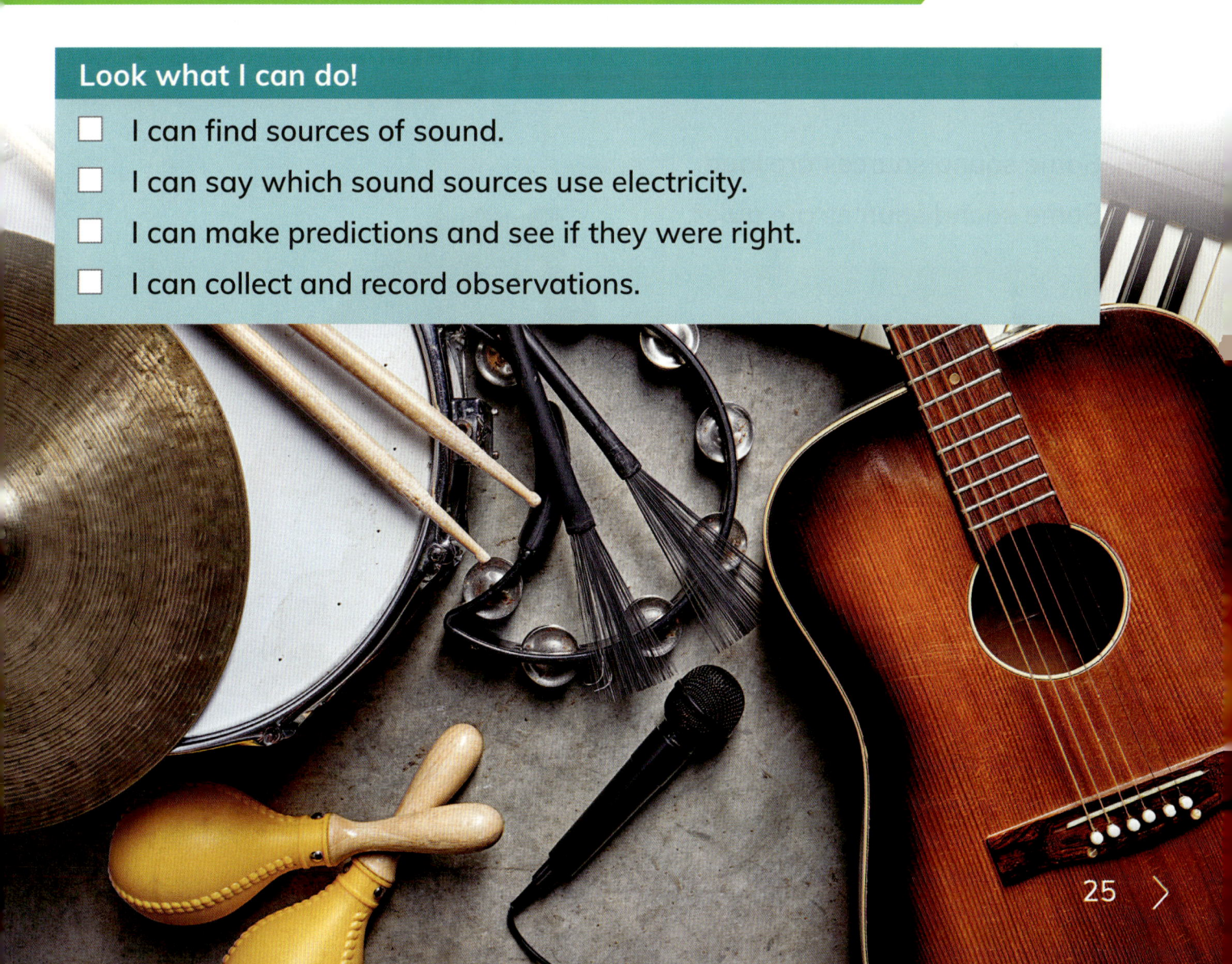

Look what I can do!

- ☐ I can find sources of sound.
- ☐ I can say which sound sources use electricity.
- ☐ I can make predictions and see if they were right.
- ☐ I can collect and record observations.

2 Sound

> 2.2 Loud and quiet

We are going to:
- learn how some sounds are loud and others are quiet
- group sounds into loud and quiet sounds
- record results in a table
- make predictions and see if they were right.

Getting started
- Talk to a friend in a quiet voice.
- Now talk to a friend in a loud voice.

damage   loud
danger   music
instruments   quiet
listen   sense

Some sound sources are **loud**.
Some sound sources are **quiet**.

A mouse makes a quiet sound.   A lion can make a loud sound.

2.2 Loud and quiet

The children are playing **instruments**.

They hear the **music** with their **sense** of hearing.

How can they play the instruments louder?

How can they play the instruments quieter?

Very loud sounds can damage your ears.

Activity 1

Grouping loud and quiet sounds

Look at the picture. Marcus is using his sense of hearing.

He can hear loud and quiet sounds.

What are they?

We can put loud sounds together in a group.

We can put quiet sounds together in a group.

27

2 Sound

Continued

Record the loud and quiet sounds from the picture like this.

We record when we draw or write something.

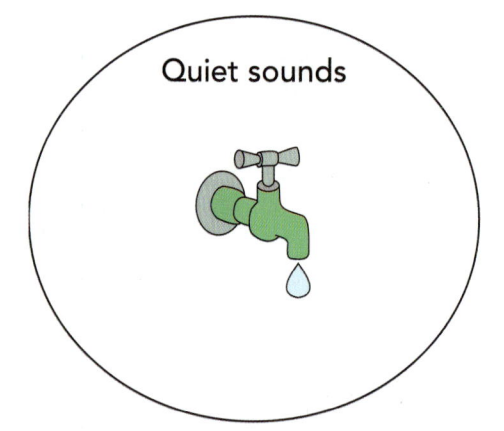

Loud sounds

Quiet sounds

Then record some sounds you can hear around you.

If you hold your hand by your ear the sound will be louder.

Tara is doing this.

She can hear more sound.

2.2 Loud and quiet

Activity 2

Make sounds louder and quieter

Ume is covering her ears.

Listen to a sound.

Now cover your ears with your hands.

What can you hear this time?

You have stopped some of the sound going into your ears.

Doing this can stop loud sounds damaging your ears.

Listen to another sound.

Now put your hand by your ear.

Does it change what you hear?

Doing this helps you hear quiet sounds.

How do your hands make things sound quieter and louder?

Think like a scientist

Do big ears help us hear?

You will need:
card, scissors, some sound sources

Some animals have large ears so they can hear sounds of **danger**.

Arun makes big card ears to see if it helps him to hear very quiet sounds.

29

2 Sound

Continued

Make some big ears and test them with your friends.

Plan which quiet sounds you will listen to.

Predict if these quiet sounds will be lounder when you use the ears.

Record your results in a table like this.

Sound source	Prediction	Result	
		It was the same	It was louder
clock	it will be louder		✓

Record your results.

Were your predictions right?

Why do the big card ears make the sounds louder?

How am I doing?

Draw two things that make a quiet sound.

Now draw two things that make a loud sound.

Activity 3

Take care of your ears!

Your ears can hear all sorts of sounds.

Your sense of hearing helps you play, learn and keep safe.

2.2 Loud and quiet

Continued

You need to take good care of our ears.

Make sure you:

- don't listen to very loud sounds
- don't stick things into your ears
- keep your ears clean.

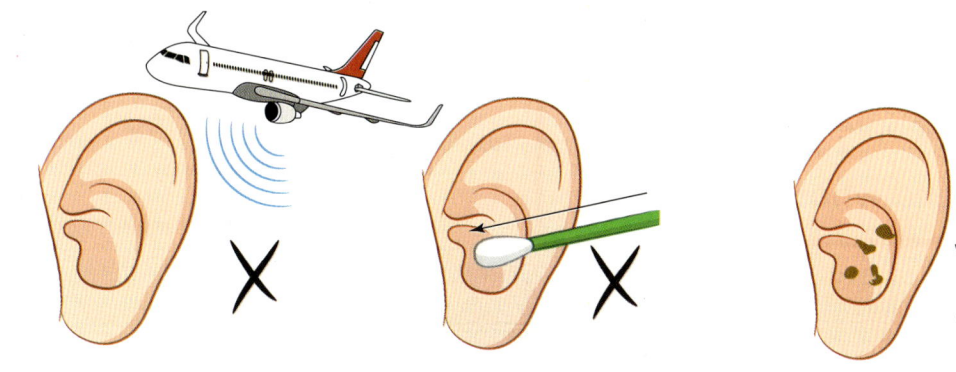

Work with a friend. Make a poster to tell all your friends how to take care of their ears.

How am I doing?

Tell a friend how to look after their ears.

When you do science, how does it help you to do the science yourself?

Look what I can do!

- ☐ I can say how some sounds are loud and others are quiet.
- ☐ I can group sounds into loud and quiet sounds.
- ☐ I can record results in a table.
- ☐ I can make predictions and see if they were right.

2 Sound

2.3 Sound moves

We are going to:
- find out how sound changes as it moves
- stay safe when we do a science investigation.

Getting started
- Can the people hear the man?
- Tell a friend what you think.

changed   move
comparing   near
far away

2.3 Sound moves

Sounds **move** away from a sound source.

We hear the sound when it gets to our ears. We call this listening.

Think like a scientist

Does sound change as it moves?

> **You will need:**
> a triangle or other instrument

The children are doing an investigation.

Who will hear a loud sound?

Who will hear a quiet sound?

They are **comparing** the sound in different places.

33

2 Sound

Continued

Try doing this science investigation.

Stand in different places and compare the sound you hear.

The sound has **changed** if it is different in different places.

Try using different sound sources.

**Do not stand near to a very loud sound. It is not safe.
It can damage your ears.**

How am I doing?

Do you hear the change in sound? Listen carefully.

Is it a big change or a small change?

Show how loud the sound is in different places with your hands.

When you are **near** to a sound source the sound is louder.

When you are **far away** from a sound source the sound is quieter

2.3 Sound moves

Activity

Near and far sounds

Arun is listening to the sound. Sofia is bringing the sound source closer.

> **You will need:**
> a sound source

Try doing this.

How does the sound change as it gets closer?

Did you find it easy to say when a sound is loud or quiet? When have you heard sounds from far away?

Look what I can do!

- [ ] I can say how sounds change when the sound source is near or far away.
- [ ] I can keep my ears safe from loud sounds.

2 Sound

Project

Making musical instruments

These people are playing music.

What musical instruments are they using?

You can make your own musical instrument.

This is a drum.

You can make a drum with a metal can, a balloon and a rubber band.

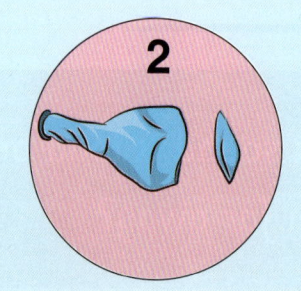

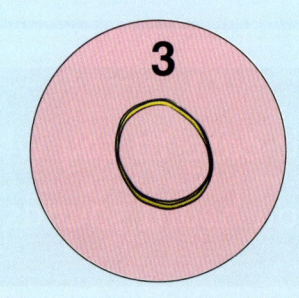

1
2
3
4
5

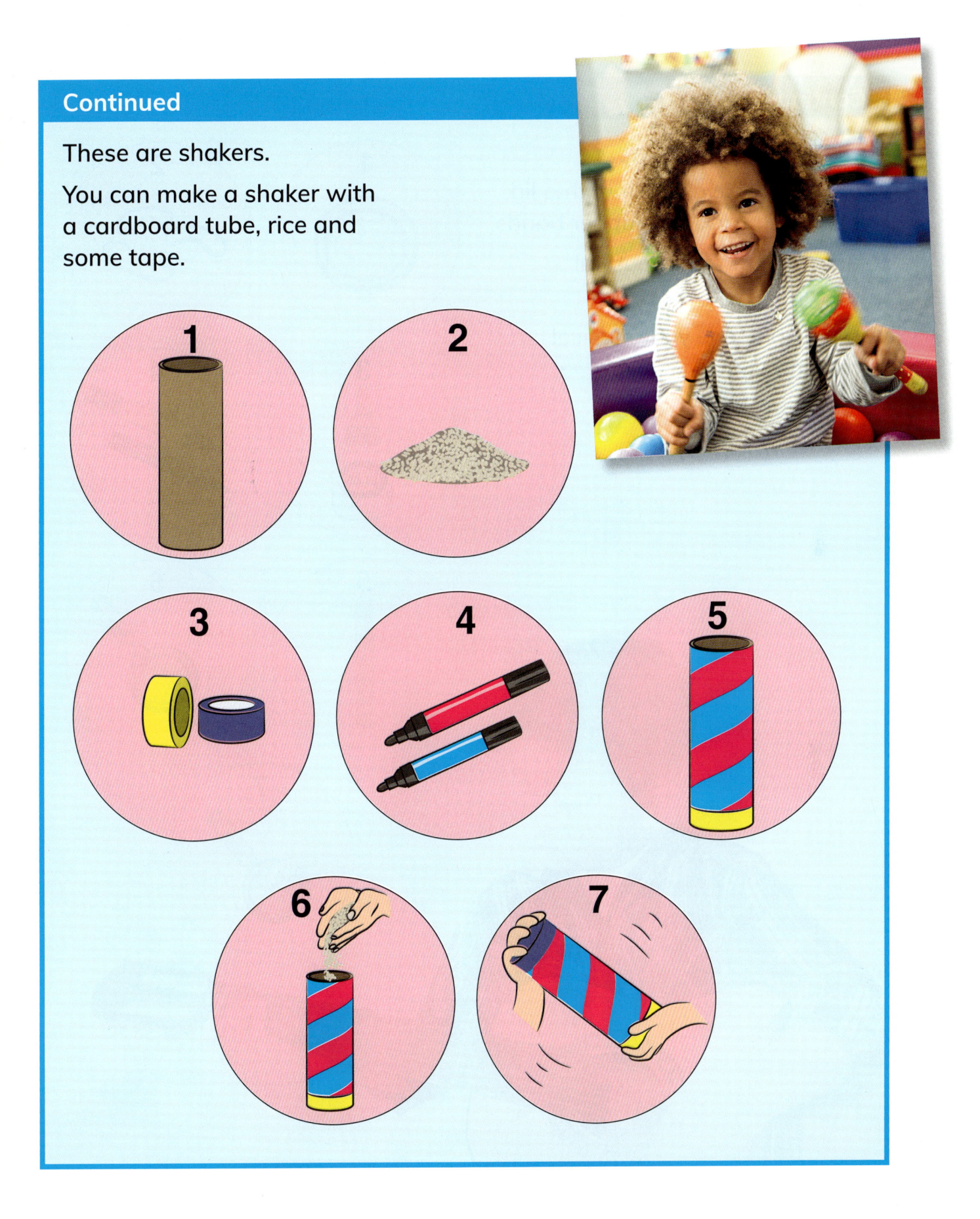

Continued

These are shakers.

You can make a shaker with a cardboard tube, rice and some tape.

37

2 Sound

Continued

This is a guitar.

You can make a guitar with a lid, a wooden stick and rubber bands.

Make one of these musical instruments.

Show someone your musical instrument.

Tell them how it works.

Check your progress

Talk about these questions.

1 Which pictures show a sound source?

2 What might happen to this girl's ears?

2 Sound

Continued

3 Which words go with which picture?

- far away
- louder
- quieter
- near

4 Ben can't hear the music.
What can he do?

3 Materials in my world

> 3.1 Different materials

We are going to:
- observe things to find out what materials they are made of
- draw things and write what they are made of.

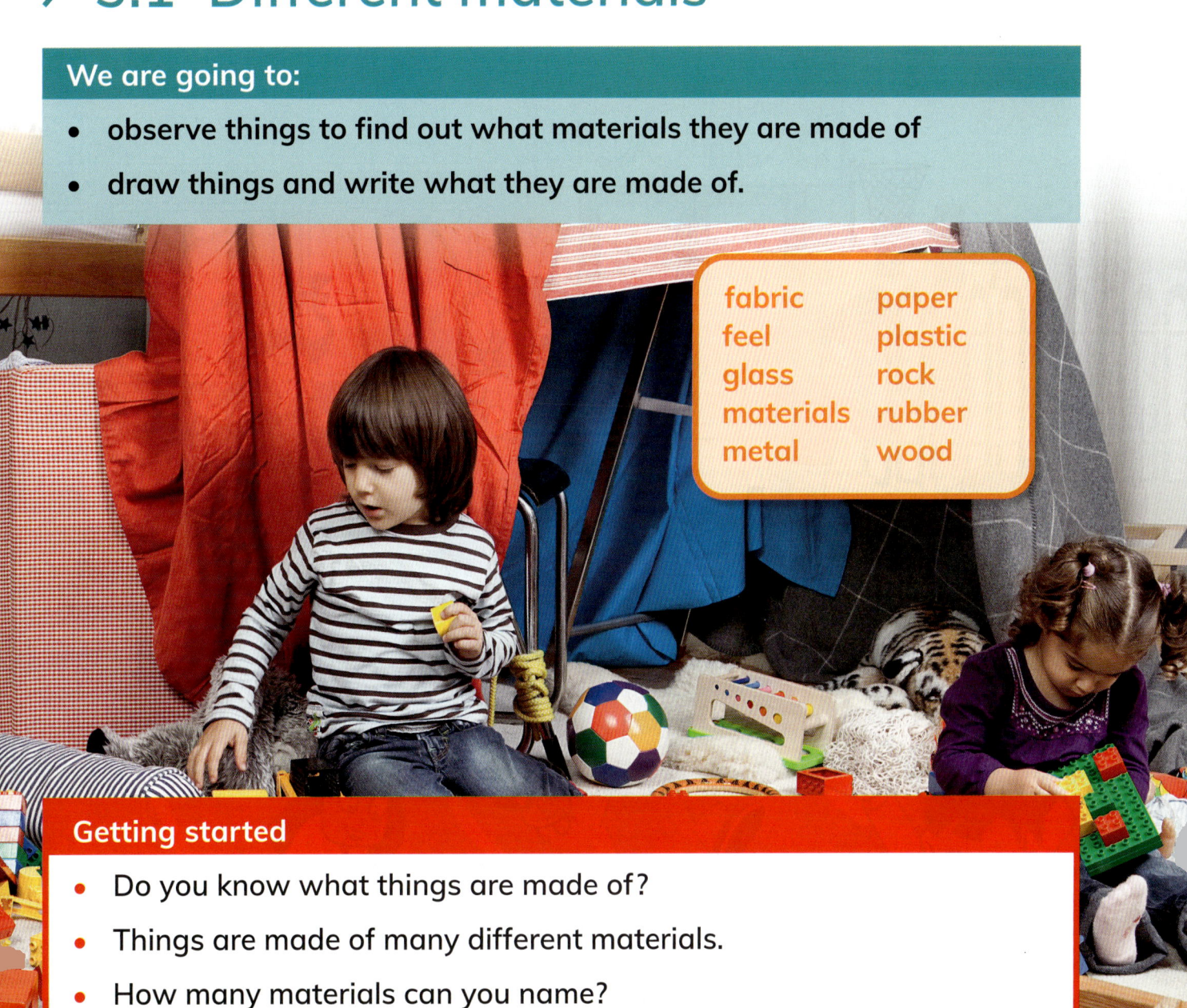

fabric   paper
feel   plastic
glass   rock
materials rubber
metal   wood

Getting started
- Do you know what things are made of?
- Things are made of many different materials.
- How many materials can you name?

3 Materials in my world

What **materials** can you see in the playground?

Can you see water, **wood**, **plastic**, **metal**, **glass**, **rock**, **paper**, **fabric** and **rubber**?

What other materials can you see?

42

3.1 Different materials

Think like a scientist

Finding materials

> You will need:
> paper and pencils, a clipboard or stiff card to lean on

Look around your classroom or school.

What are things made of?

Use your eyes. Observe carefully.

What does the material look like?

Use your hands. What does the material *feel* like?

Draw some of the things and write the name of the materials.

How am I doing?

Look at a friend's work. Have they got the materials right?

Was it easy to name the materials by looking at them?
How did the materials feel?
Tell a friend why it helped you to feel the materials.

Look what I can do!

☐ I can find and name seven or more materials.

☐ I can write words on a picture to show what I know.

43

3 Materials in my world

3.2 Properties of materials

We are going to:
- **find out about the properties of materials**
- **observe materials to find out their properties.**

Getting started
- Look around you. Feel some materials.
- Tell your friends how the material feels.

dull
flexible
hard
property
rigid
rough
shiny

smooth
soft
sort
strong
threads
weak

This metal is **strong**.

This paper is **weak**.

This wood is **hard**.

This fabric is **soft**.

This plastic is **flexible**.

This wood is **rigid**.

This metal is **shiny**.

This paper is **dull**.

Strong, weak, hard and soft are **properties** of materials.
Flexible, rigid, shiny and dull are different properties.

3.2 Properties of materials

Activity

Using materials

Look at the house. What materials can you see?

Point to some clothes.

Clothes are made from fabric.
Many fabrics are soft and flexible.

What would metal clothes be like?

What other materials have been used?
What properties do they have?

Draw something from the picture.

Write the name of the material.

Write or talk about some properties of the material.

45

3 Materials in my world

thread

Some fabrics are **rough**.

Some fabrics are **smooth**.

Look at some fabrics and feel the **threads** the fabrics are made from. Rough fabrics have bigger threads.

Think like a scientist

Rough and smooth fabrics

> **You will need:**
> four different fabrics,
> a magnifying glass

Observe some different fabrics. Which are rough? Which are smooth?

Look closely with a magnifying glass.

Feel the fabrics.

Sort the fabrics. Put them in order from rough to smooth.

How am I doing?

Have your friends put the fabrics in the same order?

3.2 Properties of materials

Which material is the best?
Is it water?

Did you find it easy to put the fabrics in order?
Which fabrics were not easy to sort?
Why were they not easy?

Look what I can do!
- ☐ I can name some properties of materials.
- ☐ I can observe materials to find out their properties.

3 Materials in my world

3.3 Sorting materials

We are going to:
- sort materials into groups
- test materials to find out their properties
- ask questions about the properties of materials.

Earth   testing
planet   waste
recycle

Getting started
- Look at some things in your classroom.
- Put things that are similar into groups. Give each group a name.

48

The planet we live on is called Earth.

When we recycle materials we can use them again.

When we recycle we make less waste.

Recycling is one way to look after planet Earth.

This plastic bottle can be recycled. It could be made into another bottle.

The paper can be recycled to make new paper.

The children are sorting waste materials into groups.

What materials can you see?

What groups would you make?

Which of these materials could be used again?

The fabric of the clothes can be used to make new clothes.

This girl has sorted her materials.

Which materials can you see?

3 Materials in my world

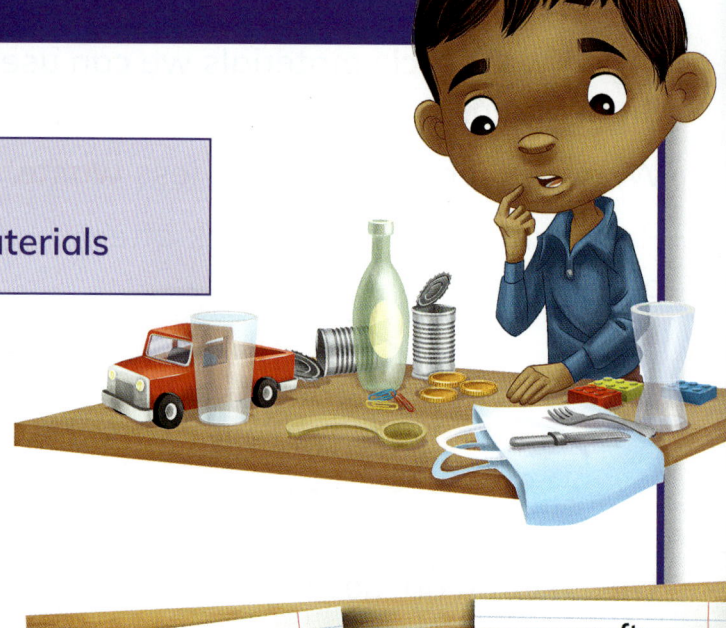

Think like a scientist

Sorting materials by observing

> **You will need:**
> some things made of different materials

Sort the materials.

Put all the metal things in a group.

Put all the plastic things in a group.

What other groups can you make?

Some metal things can be sharp.
Be careful when touching them.

There are different ways to sort materials.

Are these things in the right groups?

Which group does the spoon go in?

Make some groups like this.

Put all your hard things in one group.
Put all your soft things in a different group.

Now put all your rough things in one group.
Put all your smooth things in a different group.

What other groups can you make?

How am I doing?

Ask a friend to look at your groups. Have you put things in the right groups?

Now look at a friend's groups.

3.3 Sorting materials

Think like a scientist 2

Sorting materials by testing

You will need:
some things made of different materials

Some materials are flexible.   Some materials are rigid.

These children are **testing** materials to find out more about them.

They are finding the answer to a question:
'**Which materials are flexible?**'

What question could you ask about materials?

How could you test your materials to find out?

Use what you find out to make new groups.

Think of other tests that you could do.

51

3   Materials in my world

You have put materials into groups by observing.

You have put materials into groups by testing.

How are observing and testing different? Talk about it with your teacher.

Did you find observing or testing easier? Tell a friend.

Look what I can do!

☐   I can put similar materials in groups.

☐   I can put materials with similar properties in groups.

☐   I can test materials to find out which properties they have.

☐   I can ask questions about the properties of materials.

> 3.4 Changing materials

We are going to:
- find out which materials we can stretch, compress, twist or bend
- measure how far rubber bands stretch
- make predictions and say if we were right.

Getting started

Talk to a friend.
- Name some materials that are flexible.
- Name some materials that are rigid.

bent
compressed
elastic
measure
shapes
stretched
twisted

The football is round.
The paper is flat. They have different **shapes**.

53

3 Materials in my world

We can change the shape of most materials.

Most materials can be stretched, compressed, twisted or bent.

How is this toy being changed?

3.4 Changing materials

Activity

Changing the shape of materials

You will need:
some flexible materials and some rigid materials

Take a material. Try to change its shape.

Try to stretch it.

Try to compress it.

Try to twist it.

Try to bend it.

Record your results like Marcus has.

Which materials would not change shape? These materials are rigid.

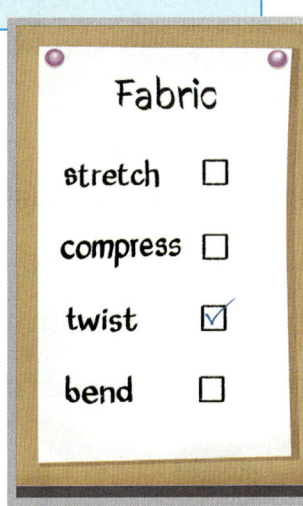

Fabric
- stretch ☐
- compress ☐
- twist ☑
- bend ☐

Materials that stretch and then go back to their old shape are called *elastic*.

Rubber is an elastic material.

The rubber rope keeping this woman safe is elastic.

55

3 Materials in my world

Think like a scientist

Which rubber band stretches most?

You will need:
some rubber bands, small bricks, a paperclip, string, a pot or small bag, some stones or marbles, a stick or wooden ruler, two chairs

Investigate this question:
'Which rubber band stretches most?'

Look at the pictures to see what to do.

Predict which rubber band will stretch most.

Count the bricks to **measure** how far different rubber bands stretch.

How am I doing?

Check your friend's measuring.

Have they counted the right number of bricks?

Which rubber band stretched the most?

Was your prediction right?

Project

Measuring is a good way to compare things.
Why is it better than just looking?

Look what I can do!

- [ ] I can name some materials that can be stretched, compressed, twisted or bent.
- [ ] I can use bricks to measure how long things are.
- [ ] I can say if my prediction was right.

Project

Reusing materials

When waste materials are not put in the bin or recycled they become litter.

You can find litter in many places, on land and in the sea.

Litter is bad for people, animals and plants.

You can recycle materials, or you can use them to make something new. You can reuse them.

What is this plant pot made from?

57

3   Materials in my world

Continued

What can you make from used materials?

Here are some ideas.

Recycle here

This sign is made from a plastic bottle, sand, a stick and used cardboard.

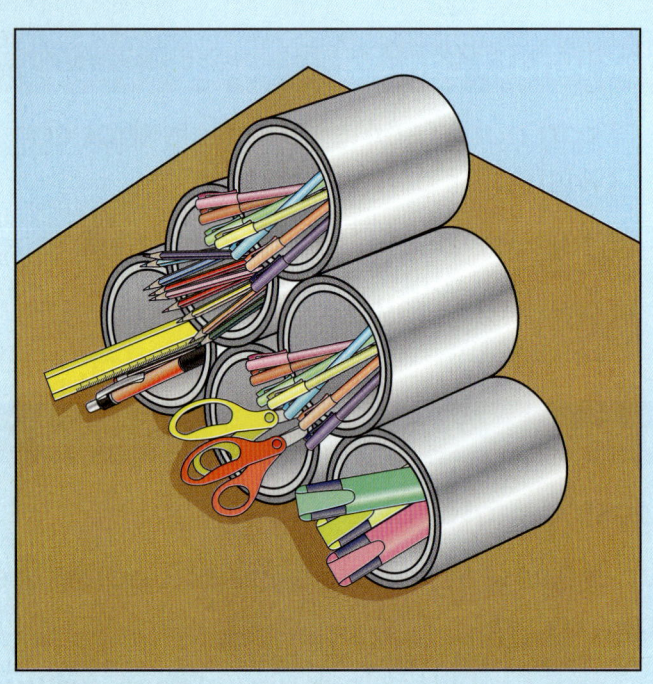

These pen holders are made from used metal cans.

This toy is made from used cardboard and plastic.

Make something from used materials.

Tell a friend why it is good for the world around us to reuse materials.

Check your progress

Talk about these questions.

1 Which recycling bins do these things go in?

2 Are these children right?

> The tyres are made of rubber because it grips well.

> The tyres are made of rubber because it is slippery.

> The tyres are made of rubber because rubber is black.

> The tyres are made of rubber because it can't hurt you.

3 **Materials in my world**

Continued

3 Which of these has been stretched, compressed, twisted and bent?

4 Look at these rubber bands.

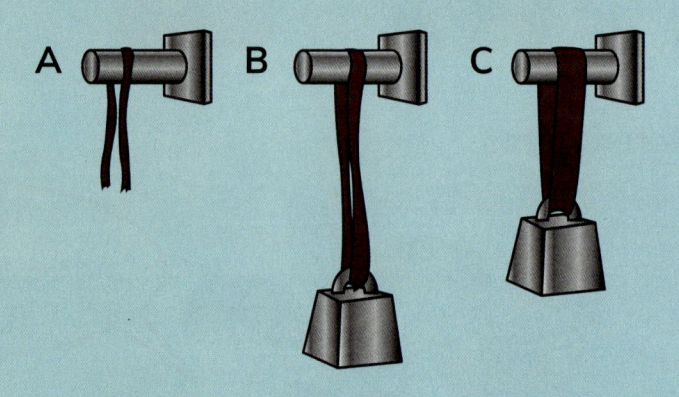

Which rubber band has stretched the longest?

Which rubber band is weak?

Which rubber band is strong?

4 ▶ The Earth

> 4.1 Planet Earth

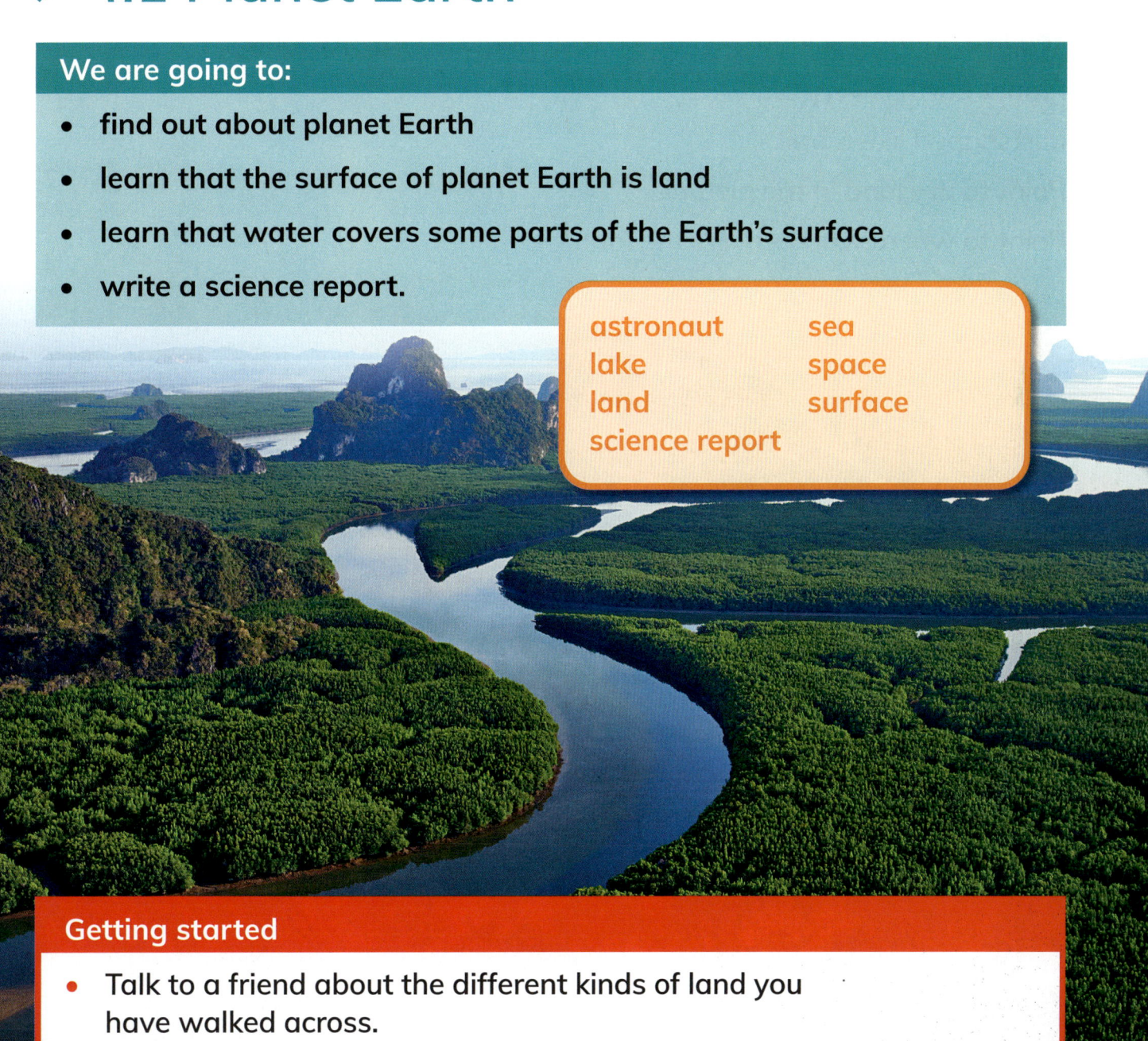

We are going to:
- find out about planet Earth
- learn that the surface of planet Earth is land
- learn that water covers some parts of the Earth's surface
- write a science report.

astronaut   sea
lake   space
land   surface
science report

Getting started
- Talk to a friend about the different kinds of land you have walked across.
- Ask your friend about the nearest water. Is it a river? A **lake**? The **sea**?

4 The Earth

Look at this picture of planet Earth.

Some parts of the **surface** of Earth are dry **land**, but some parts are covered by water.

You live on planet Earth.

You live on the dry land. You make your home on the dry land.

Planet Earth is very big.

It is shaped like a ball.

Point to dry land in the picture.

Point to where water covers the land.

4.1 Planet Earth

Activity 1

The Earth is a big ball

The Earth is so big that when you look around you cannot see that it is like a ball.

Arun and Zara cannot tell that the Earth is a ball.

Look out of the window with your friends.

Draw the window and something you can see outside.

Talk about why you cannot see the shape of the Earth.

Meg is an astronaut.

She flies so high that she goes into space.

She can see the Earth is shaped like a ball.

I can look down on planet Earth. It looks like a large ball.

63

4 The Earth

Earth is the only planet with life on it.

Talk to your friend about planet Earth and how it gives you all the things you need.

Activity 2

You are an astronaut!

You are going to write a science report to say what it is like on planet Earth.

Complete the sentences below.

These words may help you:

ball · birds · play · trees · fish · grass · swim · people

Planet Earth is like a ball.

On Earth we have many plants like…

Planet Earth is home to animals like…

I love to see…

4.1 **Planet Earth**

> **Continued**
>
> **How am I doing?**
>
> Pretend that your friend is from another planet. Tell them about planet Earth.
>
> Draw pictures to help them learn about planet Earth.

How do pictures help you learn about science?

> **Look what I can do!**
>
> - [ ] I can talk about planet Earth.
> - [ ] I can explain that some parts of the surface of Earth are dry land, but some parts are covered by water.
> - [ ] I can write a science report.

65

4 The Earth

> 4.2 Heat and light from the Sun

We are going to:
- find out about the Sun as a star
- talk about the Sun as a source of heat and light
- ask questions about the world around us.

Getting started
- With a friend, draw a picture of a tree and an animal. Now draw the Sun in the sky.
- Why do the tree and the animal need the Sun?

> die   freeze   globe   heat   stars   Sun   sunlight

At night there are many bright lights in the sky.

Many of these lights are stars, and they are very big and very hot.

But they are very, very far away.

So they look small.

4.2 Heat and light from the Sun

light

heat

One star is much closer to planet Earth.

This star is the **Sun**.

The Sun gives the **heat** and light we need.

Never look at the Sun. It will hurt your eyes.

Light from the Sun comes to planet Earth.

The light helps plants grow.

You use the light to see what you are doing.

Light from the Sun keeps the Earth warm.

4 The Earth

Without the Sun, planet Earth would be dark all the time.

Look at the pictures.

Could you do these things without light from the Sun?

4.2 Heat and light from the Sun

Activity 1

Why do we need the Sun's light?

Plants need sunlight to grow.

Look at the picture.

What would happen to plants without light from the Sun?

What would happen to animals without light from the Sun?

Draw the picture but without the light from the Sun that keeps us warm.

Talk about your drawing with a friend.

4 The Earth

Activity 2

Why do we need the Sun's heat?

Without the Sun, the Earth would be very cold.

Water would **freeze**.

Plants and animals would **die**.

Talk to a friend about what would happen to these living things without the light from the Sun keeping the Earth warm.

4.2 Heat and light from the Sun

Think like a scientist

Make a model of the Sun and the Earth

> **You will need:**
> a globe of planet Earth, a flashlight

Marcus and Arun have a **globe** of planet Earth.

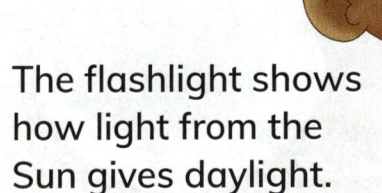

The flashlight shows how light from the Sun gives daylight.

Be careful not to shine the flashlight in someone's eyes. It could hurt their eyes.

Talk about the light from the Sun.

What questions do you have?

How does the model help you answer them?

Say what you do during the day.

Say what you do at night.

How am I doing?

Tell your friend about how the Sun can hurt you.

Ask your friend to tell you why you need the Sun.

4 The Earth

What helps you to learn about planets and stars?
Is it talking? Is it pictures?
How do these help you?

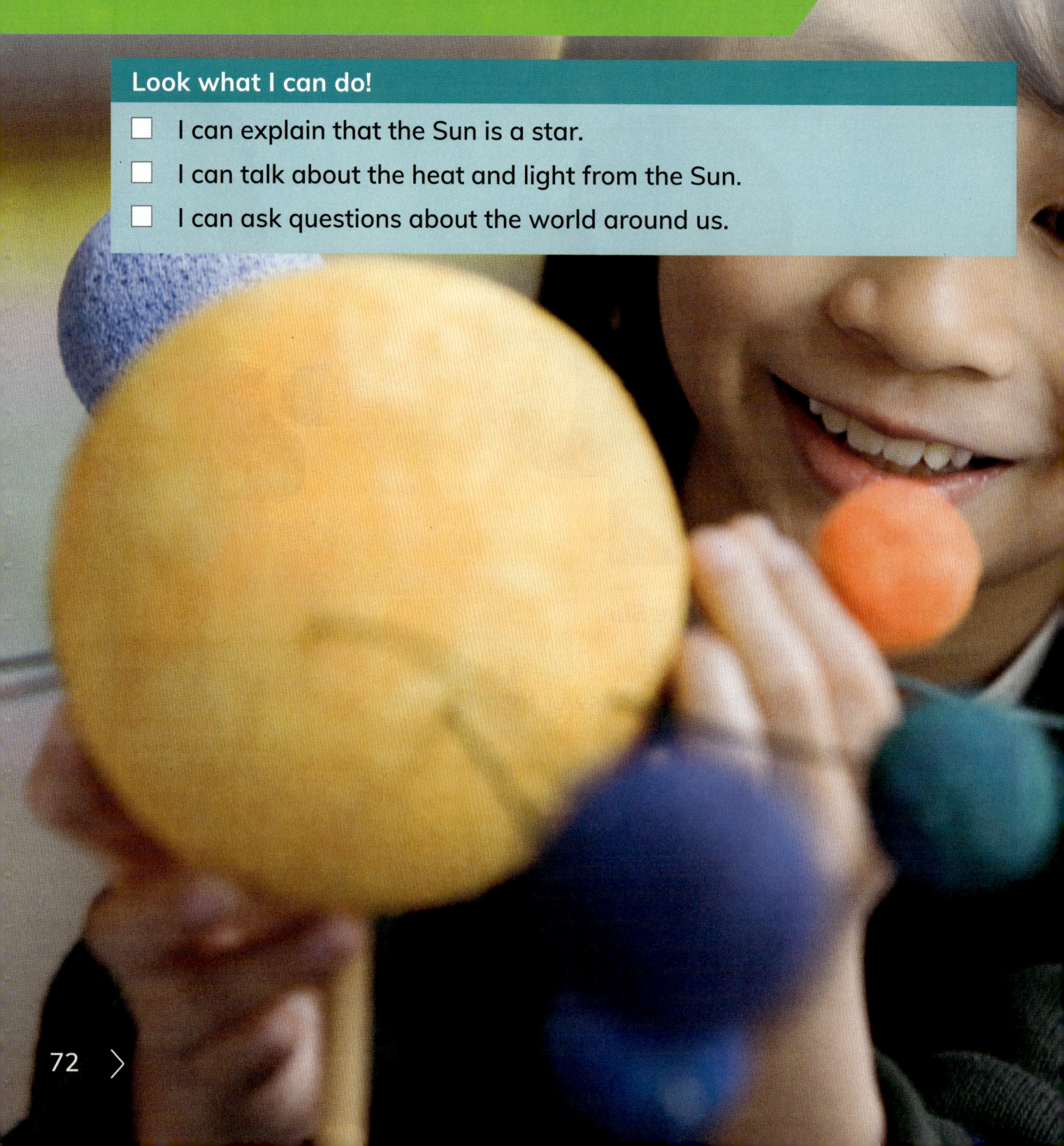

Look what I can do!
- ☐ I can explain that the Sun is a star.
- ☐ I can talk about the heat and light from the Sun.
- ☐ I can ask questions about the world around us.

> 4.3 Rocks

We are going to:

- learn that water covers most of the Earth
- learn that land is made of rock and soil
- investigate rocks by observing and sorting them
- make predictions and see if they are right.

Getting started

- Tell a friend about rocks you have seen in the ground, in a wall or a path. What were the rocks like?

The Earth is made of rocks.

You see rocks on the surface of the land.

It is not so easy to see the rocks under the water.

dry   soil
quarry   wet

4 The Earth

Some rocks are very big and some are very small.

Stones are small rocks.

Sand is made of very small pieces of rock.

Many rocks are deep beneath the surface of the Earth.

People dig out rocks in a place called a **quarry**.

They use tools and diggers to get the rocks.

4.3 Rocks

Activity

Observing and sorting rocks

This scientist studies rocks.

You can be scientists, too. Look at these pictures of rocks.

Quartz – white and clear

Granite – pink and black

Diamond – clear and shiny

Slate – grey or purple

75

4   The Earth

Continued

Sandstone – red or pink

Chalk – white

Sort the rocks into groups.

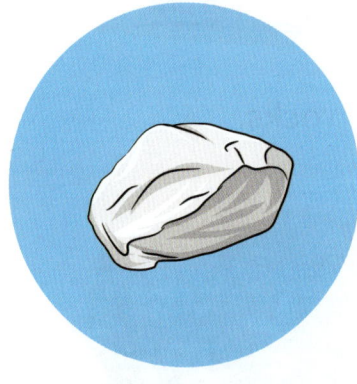

White rocks or rocks you can see through

Grey rocks

Red rocks

How are we doing?

Look at the pictures of the rocks. Which rock do you like best?

Tell a friend about your favourite rock but do not say the name. Ask your friend to point to your favourite rock.

Now ask them to tell you about their favourite rock.

4.3 Rocks

Think like a scientist 1

Making rocks wet

> **You will need:**
> rocks, water

You are going to do an investigation about rocks.

Look at some dry rocks. Feel them.

Talk about what you observe.

Point to the rocks in this picture that are wet.

How will your rocks look after getting wet?

How will your rocks feel after getting wet?

Predict what will happen.

"It's dry and hard."

"I will observe the rock with my eyes and my fingers."

Now put water on the rocks.

How does each rock change?

How does it look? How does it feel?

Were your predictions right?

4 The Earth

Look at this climber on the rock.

Why do they need dry rock to climb?

Have you ever slipped on wet rock?

Think like a scientist 2

What is on the sea floor?

On the land we see rocks, soil, animals and plants.

This scientist is observing the floor of the sea.

Predict what we might see on the sea floor if we look under the water.

Draw what you might see on the sea floor.

Look what I can do!

- ☐ I can say that the land is made of rocks.
- ☐ I can do an investigation about rocks.
- ☐ I can make predictions and see if they are right.

4.4 Soil

We are going to:
- see that the land is made of rocks and soil
- understand that soil contains living things
- draw what we find in the soil
- make predictions.

Getting started
- Talk to a friend about places where you see soil.
- Talk about how people use soil.

The surface of the land can be made of soil.

Food for humans and food for animals grows in soil.

This plant is growing in soil. Point to the roots.

You can see bits of rock in the soil.

earthworms   pattern

4 The Earth

Soil is made of bits of rock, living things and living things that have died.

You can find soil if you dig a hole.

You can find soil in a plant pot.

4.4 Soil

Activity

Observing soil

You will need:
a magnifying glass

Look very carefully at some soil.

Use a magnifying glass.

Look for roots, rocks, living things and dead things.

Draw a picture to show these things.

Earthworms help to make soil.

Without earthworms there would not be soil.

Without soil there would be no plants and no food!

What colour are earthworms?

Look at the **pattern** on their body.

Think of a question you could ask about earthworms.

4 The Earth

What other animals can you see in this picture? What plants can you see?

Think like a scientist

Testing soil

You will need:
two kinds of soil, a magnifying glass, water in two bowls

You are going to investigate two kinds of soil.

Do they look the same?

Do they feel the same?

Predict: will you find rock in the soils?

4.4 Soil

Continued

Add a little of each soil into each bowl of water.

Stir the water.

Do you see stones and sand? This is rock.

What else can you see in the soil?

Draw what you observe.

What differences have you seen between the soils?

Make sure you wash your hands after touching the soil.

How am I doing?

Tell a friend the words you can use now when you talk about soil.

How does a magnifying glass help you learn about the things in soil?

Look what I can do!

☐ I can say that land is made of rock and soil.
☐ I know that soil contains living things.
☐ I can draw what I find in soil.
☐ I can make predictions.

83

4 The Earth

Project

Scientists learn about planets

"In the past scientists thought the Earth was flat."

"Some thought that people could fall off the edge of the Earth."

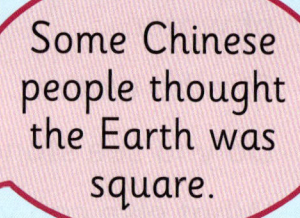

"Some Chinese people thought the Earth was square."

Long ago, some people thought the world rested on four elephants and the elephants stood on a giant turtle.

Scientists now know that these old ideas are wrong. The planets and Sun are all like large balls.

About 400 years ago, a scientist called Galileo made a telescope to observe the Moon and planets better.

The telescope makes things look bigger so that you can see them better.

Continued

Now telescopes are bigger and can see much more.

This very big telescope is in space!

Make a poster to show a scientist from long ago and one from today talking.

On your poster, draw a speech bubble and write in it the words that today's scientist would say.

I think the Earth is flat.

Make a model to show the Earth is like a ball.

Draw the land and sea on your model.

4 The Earth

Check your progress

Talk about these questions.

1 Choose the right letter for each label.

Water covers land: A, B or C?

Land: A, B or C?

Animals dig in the soil: A, B or C?

2 Say the missing word in each sentence. Use these words.

light   heat

The _____ from the Sun keeps animals and plants warm.

Without the Sun's _____ plants would not grow.

Continued

3 Point to three things that have been made with rocks in this picture.

4 You find different things when you look at soil.

Look at this picture and name a living thing and a dead thing.

Point to a rock.

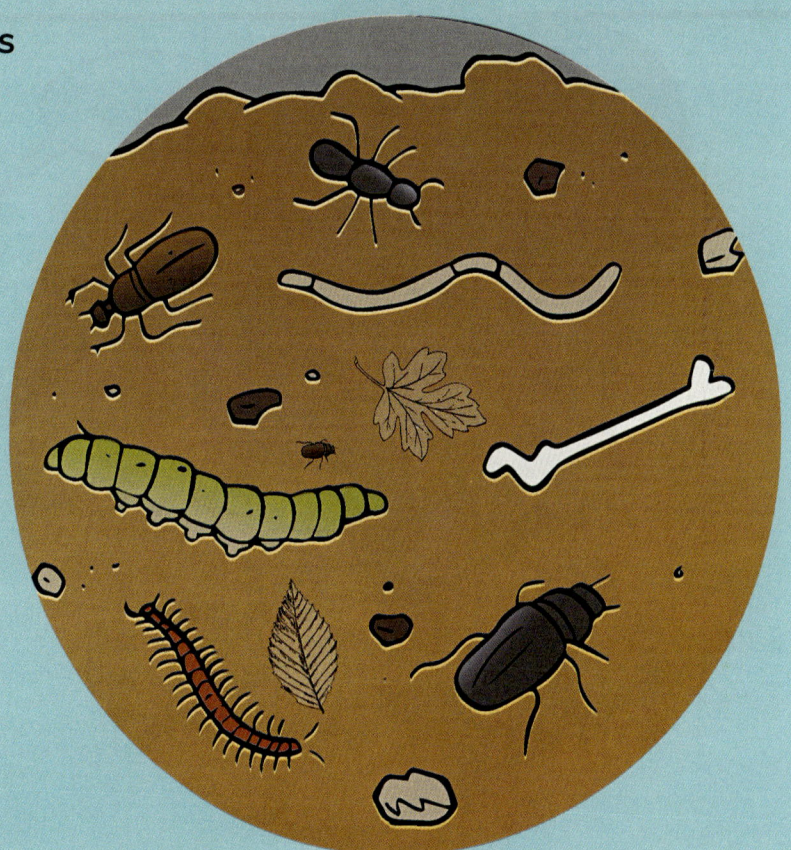

5 Humans

5.1 Our bodies

We are going to:
- name the main parts of the body
- compare bodies.

Getting started
- Look at a friend. How many body parts can you name?

body	short
human	skin
label	tall
long	

Head

5.1 Our bodies

Men, women and children are **humans**.

Human **bodies** have arms, legs, a head and other parts. Our bodies are covered in **skin**.

Look at the parts of the body.

Read the **labels**.

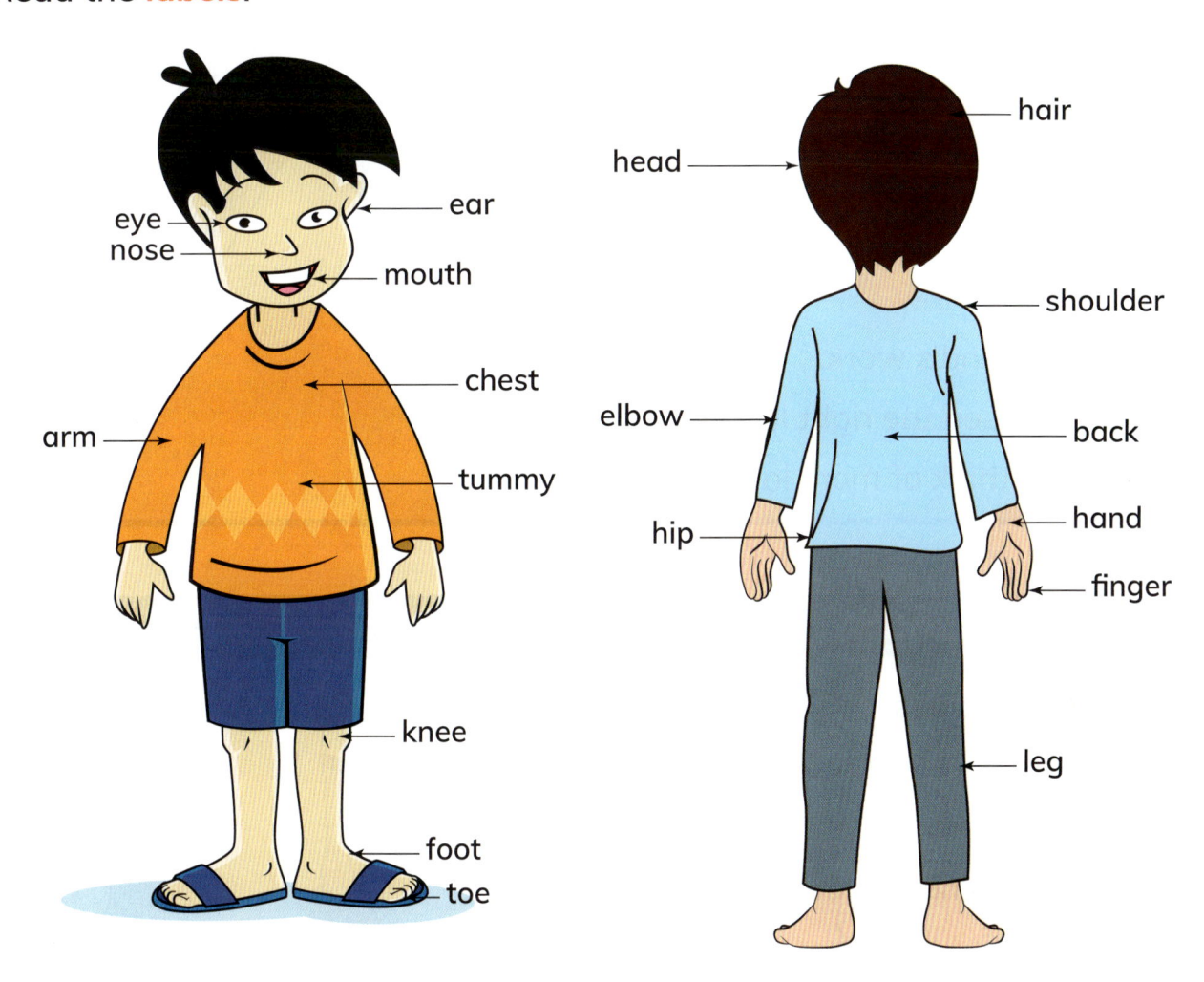

How many legs do you have?

How many fingers do you have?

What other body parts can you name?

Which part of the body is the most important? Is it the head?

Some people's bodies are different and they may need to do some things differently.

5 Humans

Activity

Parts of the body

Cut out or draw a human.

Label the human with these body parts:

head, hair, ear, mouth, arm, leg, knee, foot, hand.

What other labels could you have on the drawing?

How am I doing?

Look at a friend's work.

Have they used the right labels?

Could they think of more labels?

Think like a scientist

Comparing bodies

Are human bodies the same?

Put your foot next to a friend's foot.

Are your feet the same? Which foot is **longer**? Which foot is **shorter**?

Now compare your hands.

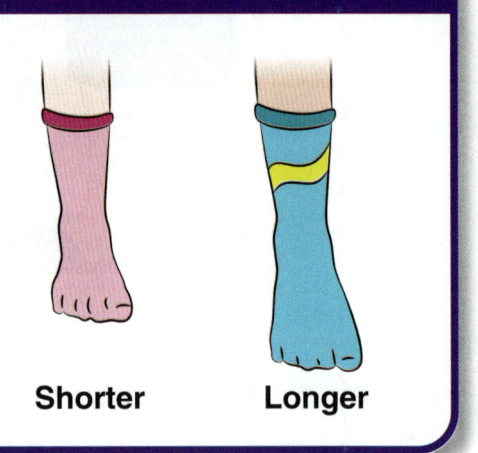

Shorter   Longer

5.1 Our bodies

Continued

Look at the picture of the two boys. Femi is **taller** than Dan.

Stand back to back with a friend like this.

Who has longer arms?

Who is taller? Who is shorter?

There are many body parts.
Would a song help you learn the names?
Do you know a song about the body?

Look what I can do!

☐ I can name many parts of the body.

☐ I can talk about how bodies are different.

5 Humans

> 5.2 Our amazing senses

We are going to:
- learn to name the five senses and say what they do
- learn the part of the body we use for each sense
- use our different senses to observe things.

Getting started
- Talk with a friend. What are our senses?
- How many senses can you name?

hearing touch
sight taste
smell

We use our senses to find out what is around us.

Humans have five senses:

- **Sight:** we use our eyes to see.
- **Hearing:** we use our ears to hear.
- **Smell:** we use our nose to smell.
- **Touch:** we use our skin to touch.
- **Taste:** we use our mouth to taste.

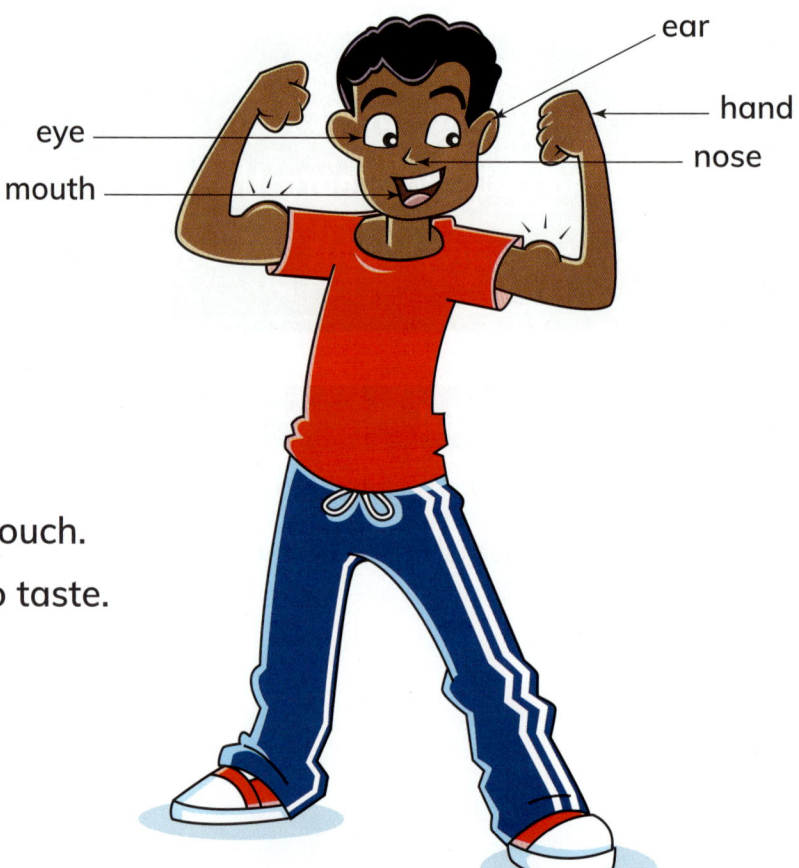

5.2 Our amazing senses

Activity

I can't see!

Sofia is playing a game. She has to put the arm on the boy.

Her eyes are covered. She cannot use her sense of sight.

Zara is telling her what to do. Sofia is using her sense of hearing.

Play this game.

You have to listen carefully.

How am I doing?

Did you listen carefully?

Was it easy to put the body parts in the right place?

5 Humans

Think like a scientist

What can you smell?

You will need:
some things that have a strong smell in pots that have lids with holes

Arun is investigating what is inside.

He is using his sense of smell to make a prediction.

Arun writes his predictions and results in a table.

	A	B	C
Prediction	coffee	orange	chocolate
Result	coffee	lemon	chocolate

Were Arun's predictions right?

Try doing this investigation.

Record your predictions and results in a table.

5.2 Our amazing senses

Do you close your eyes to use your other senses?
Does closing your eyes make it easier to smell or listen carefully?

Look what I can do!

- [ ] I can name the five senses and say what they do.
- [ ] I can name the part of the body we use for each sense.
- [ ] I can use my different senses to observe things.

5 Humans

> 5.3 Similar and different

We are going to:
- find out how humans are similar
- find out how humans are different
- make drawings to show what we observe
- sort humans into groups.

Getting started
- Find a friend. Tell them how you are similar.
- Find another friend. Tell them how you are different.

blonde   same   twins

Look at these children.

They all look similar in some ways. They all have two eyes.

They look different in other ways. They have different hair.

In what other ways are they similar?

In what other ways are they different?

5.3 Similar and different

These children are **twins**. They do not look different.

We say they look the **same**.

Do you know any twins?

> **Think like a scientist**
>
> **How are we different?**
>
> Talk to your friends about how you are different.
>
> These children have used hair colour to make groups. They have made a brown group, a black group and a **blonde** group.
>
> Make groups like this with your friends.
>
> Use one thing that is different like height, eye colour or clothes.
>
> Think of a name for each group.
>
> **How am I doing?**
>
> Look at your groups. Are all the children in the right group?
>
> How do you know?

97

5 Humans

Activity

How are we similar?

Compare how you look with a friend.

Observe your faces.

Observe your hair.

Observe your bodies.

Talk about how you look similar and how you look different.

Make drawings to show how you look similar and different.

Was it easy to make the groups?
Did you use just one thing that was different?

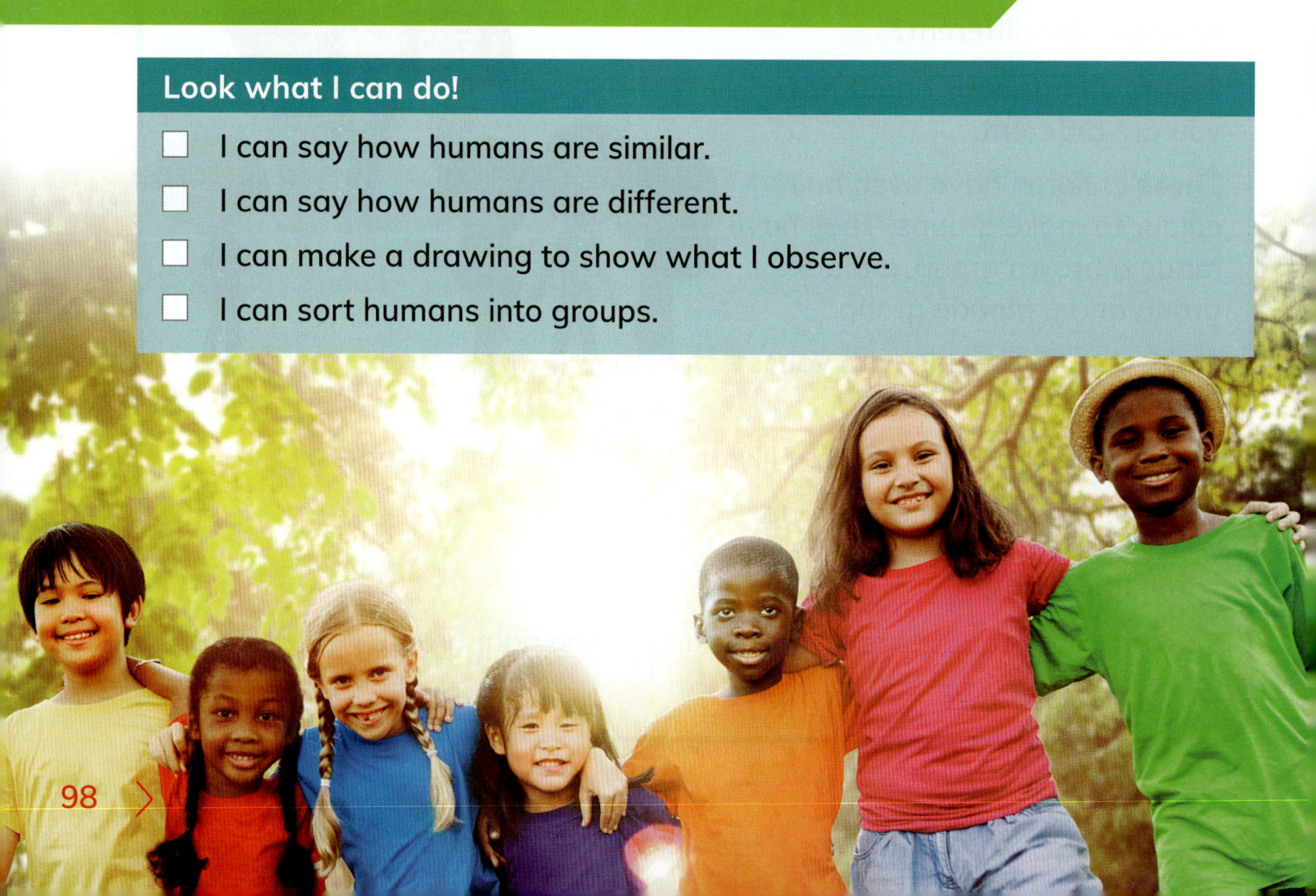

Look what I can do!

- ☐ I can say how humans are similar.
- ☐ I can say how humans are different.
- ☐ I can make a drawing to show what I observe.
- ☐ I can sort humans into groups.

5.4 Staying alive

We are going to:
- find out what humans and animals need to stay alive
- learn which food is healthy
- do an investigation and find out if our predictions are right.

Getting started

Which things does Marcus need to stay alive?
- Does he need food?
- Does he need toys?
- Does he need any other things?

air
breathe
gills
healthy
unhealthy

5 Humans

Humans and other animals need the right things to stay alive.

This woman has **air** in a bottle so she can **breathe** under water.

All animals need air to stay alive. The shark uses **gills** to breathe. Gills take in air from the water.

All animals need water to drink and the right food to stay alive.

Food that is good for humans is called **healthy** food.

Food that is not good for us is called **unhealthy** food.

healthy food

unhealthy food

5.4 Staying alive

> **Activity**
>
> **What would you take to the stars?**
>
> Sofia, Zara and Arun are going to the stars.
>
> What do they need to take with them to stay alive?
>
> Draw a picture of the things you would take to the stars to keep you alive.
>
> **How am I doing?**
>
> Look at a friend's work. Have they got water and air in their picture?
>
> Have they got healthy food in their picture?

It is good to try healthy food to find out if you like the taste.

Sam thinks he won't like kiwi fruit.

Taste this kiwi fruit. It's nice.

No. I don't like it. It's hairy.

Look it's great inside.

Hmmm.

Fruit and vegetables are good for you.

It's nice.

Sam's prediction was not right.

When our predictions are wrong, we learn something new.

Sam learnt that he likes kiwi fruit.

5 Humans

Think like a scientist

Which healthy food do you like?

> **You will need:**
> some healthy foods to taste

Try tasting some new healthy foods.

Which ones will you like?

Record your predictions and the results in a table like this.

Healthy food	Prediction Will you like it?	Result Did you like it?
pineapple	no	yes
brown bread		
carrot		

Were any of your predictions wrong? Talk about it with your friends.

Did you learn something new?

5.4 Staying alive

When our predictions are wrong, we learn something new.
Some people don't like to say when they are wrong.
When you can say when your predictions are wrong it will help you to learn.

Look what I can do!

- ☐ I can talk about three things humans and animals need to stay alive.
- ☐ I can name some healthy foods.
- ☐ I can say when my predictions are right or wrong.

5 Humans

Project

Making a healthy salad

Lin is a cook. She makes food for the children.

Lin has to make the food healthy.

Lin makes a salad. A salad is a mixture of different foods.

She uses these foods. Is her salad healthy?

noodles	tomatoes	peppers	bean sprouts	carrots

Make a healthy salad.

Draw the food you will use.

Make your salad and taste it.

Tell your friends about the healthy foods you used.

Check your progress

Check your progress

Talk about these questions.

1. **Point to these parts of the boy's body:**

   head   eyes   hair   shoulders

   nose   toes   arms   hands

5 Humans

2 Lina has her eyes closed. She cannot see.

Can she hear?

Can she taste?

Can she touch?

Can she smell?

Which body parts does she use to hear, taste, touch and smell?

3 Some children compared hair colour.

Here are the results.

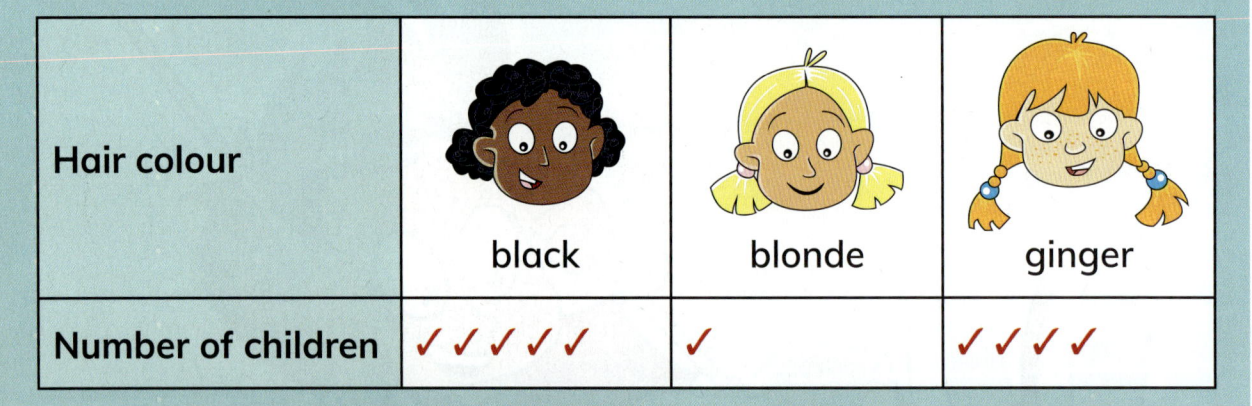

Hair colour	black	blonde	ginger
Number of children	✓✓✓✓	✓	✓✓✓

How many children had black hair?

How many had blonde hair?

How many had ginger hair?

How many children were there altogether?

Check your progress

4 Which lunch box is healthier?

5 Which of these foods are healthy?

107

6 Forces

6.1 Moving things

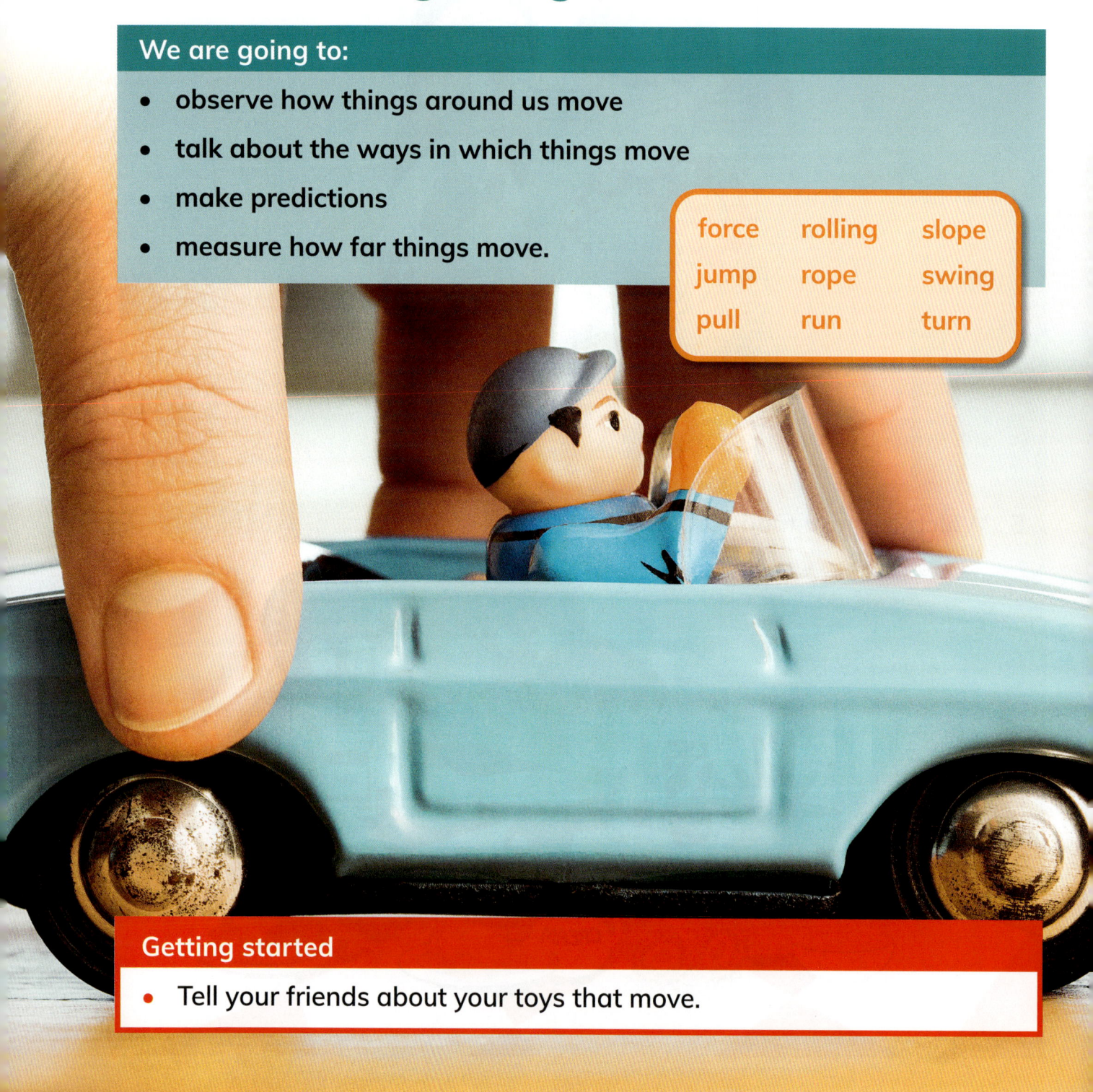

We are going to:
- observe how things around us move
- talk about the ways in which things move
- make predictions
- measure how far things move.

force	rolling	slope
jump	rope	swing
pull	run	turn

Getting started
- Tell your friends about your toys that move.

6.1 Moving things

All around us are things that move.

Look at the picture and how things move.

How does the ball move?

How does the rope move?

How do the children move?

Activity 1

Moving toys

You will need:
moving toys

Observe these toys and say how they move.

6 Forces

> **Continued**
>
> Now look at other toys.
> Observe them carefully.
> How do they move?
> Draw a picture of a toy that moves.

Some things are easy to move.

Some things are hard to move.

They all need a **force** to make them move.

Things that are small and things that are light can be easy to move.

Things that are big and things that are heavy can be harder to move.

Will these people be able to **pull** this plane?

How many children could pull a plane?

We have to take care when moving big things.

Moving things can hurt us or other people.

6.1 Moving things

Activity 2

How people move

Go outside the classroom.

Can you move slowly?

Can you move like a bird?

Find different ways to move.

swinging

running

jumping

turning

Draw a picture of yourself moving.

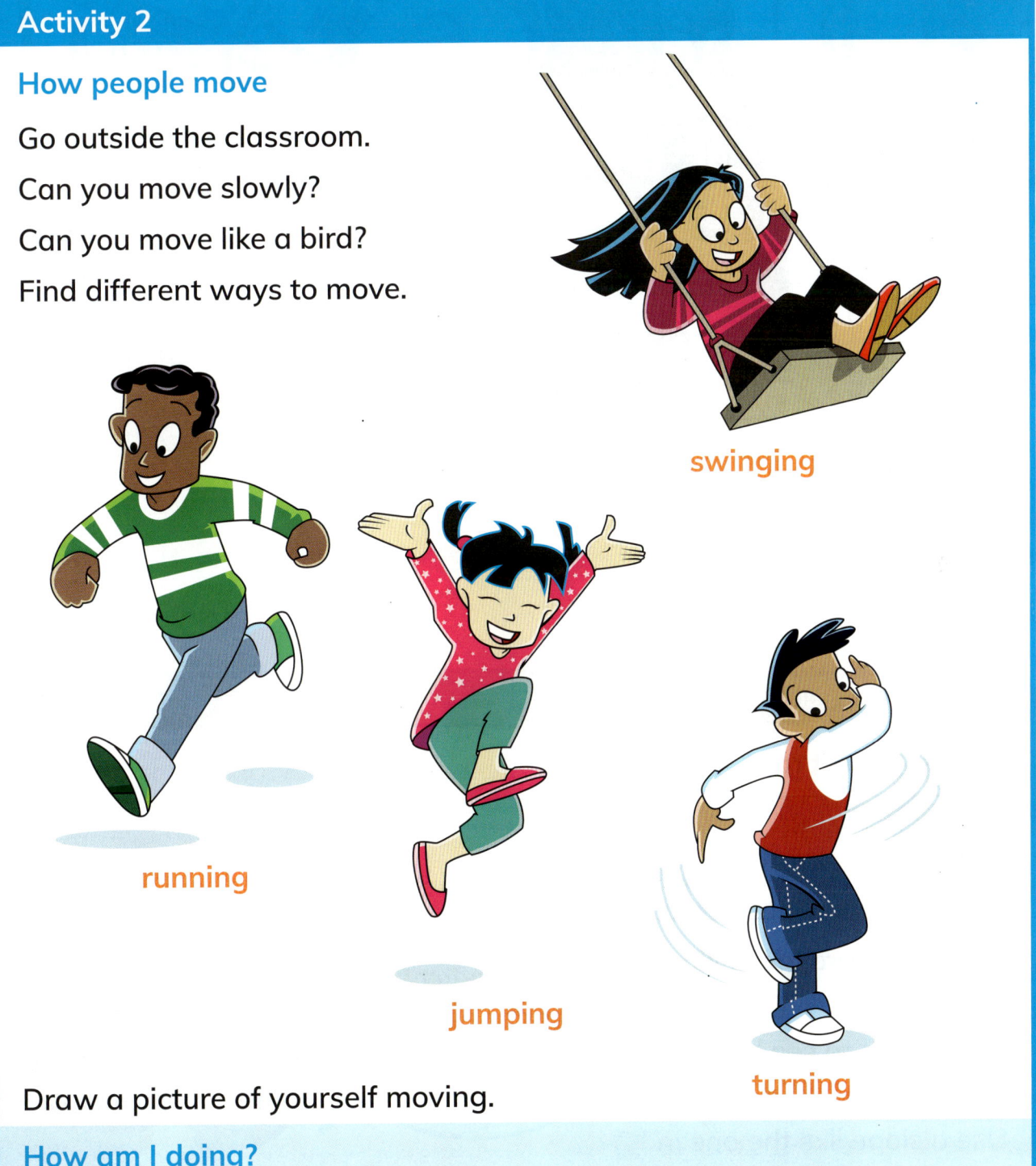

How am I doing?

Tell your friend how you move around your home.

How do you climb stairs?

How do you lie down and stand up?

6 Forces

Moving in space can be hard.

How is this astronaut moving?

Think like a scientist

How far will it roll?

You will need:
a pencil, a tube, a crayon, a roll of sticky tape, a ball

Arun and Zara are **rolling** balls down a **slope**.

Test things to see how far they roll.

Use a slope like the one in the picture.

Try things like this.

I predict that the red ball will not roll as far.

112

Continued

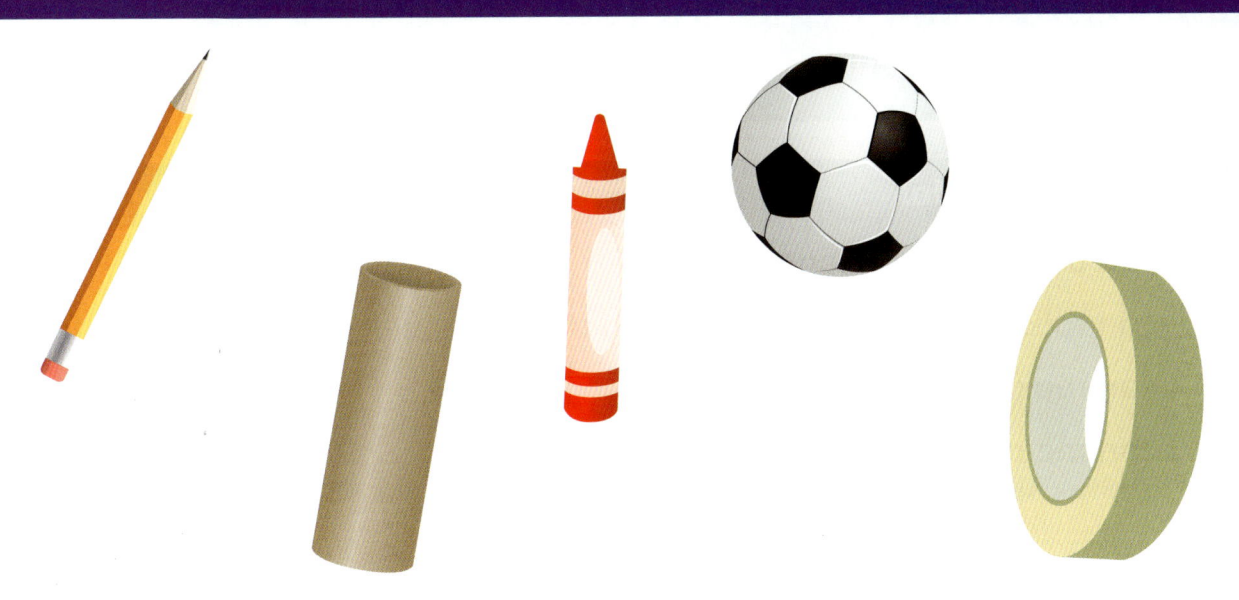

Predict how far each thing will roll.

Put each thing at the top of the slope and let go.

Measure how far it moves on the floor.

Add each result to a table like this.

	How far will it roll?	
	Prediction	Result
ball	🖐 🖐 🖐	🖐 🖐 🖐 🖐
My table: how far did things roll?		

Which rolled the furthest?

6.1 Moving things

113

6 Forces

> When I observe other children doing science, how does it help me learn science?

Look what I can do!

- ☐ I can observe how things move.
- ☐ I can talk about the ways in which things move.
- ☐ I can make predictions.
- ☐ I can measure how far things move.

> 6.2 Push and pull forces

We are going to:
- find out about pushing and pulling
- make measurements
- record observations in a table
- keep safe when doing science.

Getting started
- Show your friend something in the classroom that can be safely pulled and pushed.
- Ask them to show you a different thing we can pull or push.

This bulldozer is a **machine**. It uses a pushing force.

What other machines **push** and pull to make things move?

machine   start
push   stop
slide

115

6 Forces

We can move things with a push or pull force.

Push and pull this science book.

Think of other things you can push and pull.

Think of something that you can't push or pull.

Activity

Push or pull?

Look around your classroom.

Predict what things you can push or pull.

You will need:
sticky notes or labels saying 'push' and 'pull', things around the classroom to push and pull

Try to push and pull these things.

Were you right?

Label them with 'push' or 'pull'.

Which things did not move when you pushed or pulled them?

6.2 Push and pull forces

Why do some things not move when you push them?

Look at this picture.

Talk about the pushing force and the pulling force.

Are the forces too big or too small?

How could the children pull and push with more force?

How could another child help?

Sometimes we push or pull to **start** things moving.

To make things **stop** we sometimes pull or push.

6 Forces

Think like a scientist

How far will it slide?

You will need:
a chair, a large rubber band, bricks, large sheets of paper, sticky tape, things to slide

Adra asks: 'With the same push, how far will each thing slide?'

Adra is pulling the rubber band.

When she lets go, the rubber band will push the book.

The book will slide.

Marcus is predicting what will happen.

6.2 Push and pull forces

Continued

Speech bubble: The book will not slide as far as the box.

Now do this activity.

Take care putting the rubber band on the chair legs.

Use the rubber band to give a push to different things.

Always put the thing that you are testing at the same starting line.

Why is this important?

How far do different things slide?

Record what happens like this.

Object	How far?
box	9 bricks
pencil case	

How am I doing?

You pulled the elastic band back so that it pushed things.

Draw what would happen with a bigger elastic band pulled back more.

Explain this to a friend.

119

6 Forces

When you are doing tests, how can you keep yourself and your friends safe?

Look what I can do!

- ☐ I can say that pushes and pulls are forces.
- ☐ I can make measurements.
- ☐ I can record my observations.
- ☐ I can stay safe when doing science.

6.3 Making things move

We are going to:
- investigate small and bigger pushes
- find things that need electricity to work
- make predictions about what will happen
- record observations in a table
- describe what happened and see if it matches a prediction.

Getting started
- Draw something that is very easy to push or pull.
- Talk to a friend about why this is easy to move.

When you move, you use push and pull forces.

The skateboarder pushes with his feet.

He pulls with his hand.

cell   mains
little   tiny

6 Forces

Activity 1

Let's see the force of the push

You will need:
a balloon, a chair, a table, a drawer, a door, a box, a book

When people move it can be hard to see the force.

A balloon can help us to see a pushing force.

The girl is pushing with a balloon.

This shows us how hard she is pushing.

Use a balloon to push things in class.

Take care! Can you show others how hard you are pushing?

Now we can use a balloon to show **tiny** pushes, **little** pushes and bigger pushes.

Use a balloon to push things.

Start with a tiny push, then push a little harder.

6.3 Making things move

Continued

Try pushing these things with a balloon.

Does the balloon help to show the push?

Now record your pushing on a table like this.

Object	Tiny push	Little push	Bigger push
chair	it did not move	it did not move	it moved

123

6 Forces

Think like a scientist

Measure the push and the slide

You will need:
a chair, sticky tape, a large rubber band, large sheets of paper, bricks, objects to slide

In Topic 6.2 you used a rubber band to give things a pushing force.

If you pull harder on the rubber band you give a bigger pushing force.

Try this now.

Choose some things to push with the rubber band.

Predict any things that will not move with just a little push.

Give each thing a little push, a bigger push and a biggest push.

Record your results like this.

Thing	Little push	Bigger push	Biggest push
pen	4 bricks	6 bricks	9 bricks

Was your prediction right?

6.3 Making things move

Electricity can make things move.

Many things that move don't need electricity.

But some things need electricity to make them move.

Some things use electric **cells**, others use **mains** electricity.

This toy car has electric cells.

The food mixer uses mains electricity.

Electricity makes the toy car and the food mixer move.

Take care! You should not touch mains powered plugs and wires.

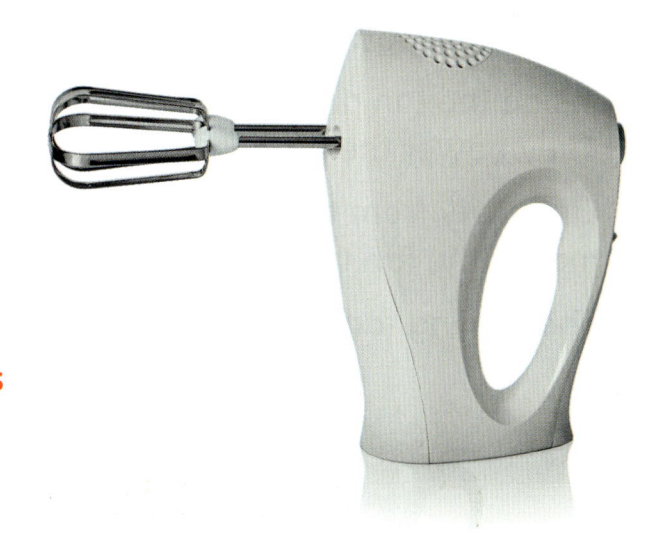

125

6 Forces

Activity 2

Electricity can make things move

Look around your classroom and school.

Record things that need electricity.

Do they use electric cells or mains electricity?

Record your observations like this.

Machine	Mains	Cell	Makes things move
food mixer	✓		✓

Activity 3

Electricity can make air move

This fan is powered by cells.

Inside the fan are two cells. They power the fan.

Electricity from the cells makes the fan turn.

The turning fan pushes air.

6.3 Making things move

Continued

The moving air will make things move.

Have a look at a fan and its electric cells.

Can you switch the fan on and off?

Will the electric fan make things move?

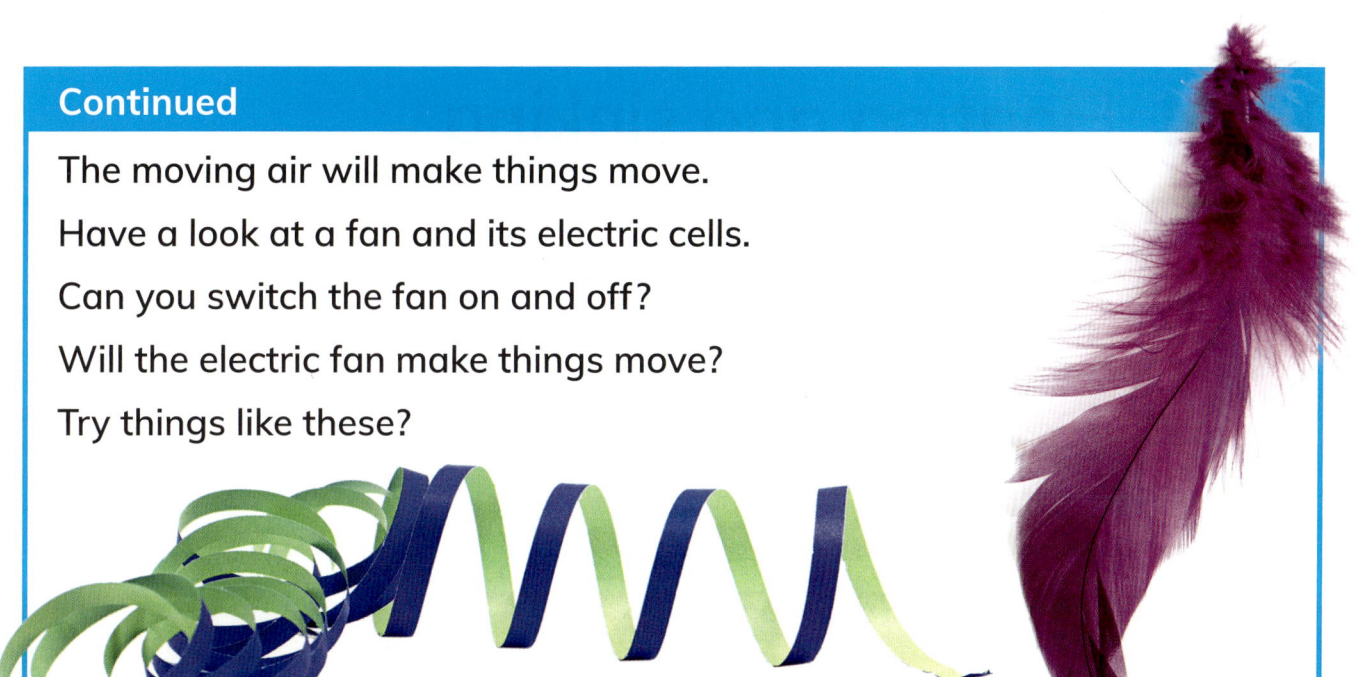

Try things like these?

How am I doing?

Ask your friend to name some things in your classroom that can be pushed or pulled.

Are they right?

Tell your friend how to measure pushes and how far things move.

If your prediction is wrong, does this matter?

Look what I can do!

- ☐ I can investigate small and bigger pushes.
- ☐ I can find things that need electricity to work.
- ☐ I can make predictions about what will happen.
- ☐ I can record my observations in a table.
- ☐ I can describe what happened and say if it matches my prediction.

6 Forces

> 6.4 Floating and sinking

We are going to:

- see that some objects float and others sink
- sort and group objects
- record observations in a table
- make predictions.

Getting started

- Draw something that floats and something that sinks.

Some things **float** in water.

Lots of things **sink** in water.

Look at the picture. What things sink?

float   sink

6.4 Floating and sinking

Activity 1

Will it float?

You will need:
a bowl of water, things that will float, things that will sink

Make a group of things that you predict will float.

Make a group of things that you predict will sink.

Put them in groups like this.

Test the things using a bowl of water.

Do they float or sink?

Record your predictions and results like this.

Object	Predict	Test
ball	it will float	it floated

6 Forces

Activity 2

Make it float

You will need:
modelling clay, bowl of water

Will this ball of clay sink or float?

Predict what will happen.

Test it in water.

Does it float?

We can change some things that sink to make them float.

Try to change the shape of the clay to make it float.

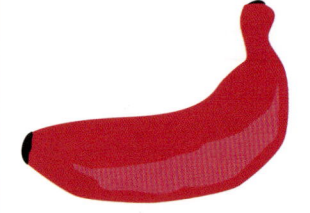

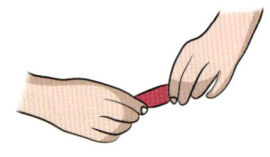

Test different clay shapes to see if they will float.

Predict what will happen.

What did you find?

Which new shapes float?

6.4 Floating and sinking

Look at the things that sink.

Try to say why they sink.

Look at the things that float.

Try to say why they float.

Some materials, like wood, float on water.

Some things filled with air float on water.

Try to say why these giant balls float on the water.

Always take care near deep water, it can be very dangerous.

Think like a scientist

Air helps things float

> **You will need:**
> a balloon, a beach ball, a football, a plastic bottle half full of water, another plastic bottle almost full of water, a tank or bucket of water

Sofia knows that air can help things to float.

Sofia wants to test some things to see if they float.

All of them have air inside them.

Predict which things will float.

Record your predictions.

Now test to see which things float.

Record your results in a table, like the one on the next page.

131

6 Forces

Continued

Object	Will it float?	
	Prediction	Draw what happened
balloon	🙂	

What do you notice about the ways that different things float?

Do you think that air helps them float?

How am I doing?

Point to things that float and sink.

Draw two things that float and two things that sink.

If you see something new, do you wonder what it is? Do you ask questions about it?

Look what I can do!

☐ I can test things to see if they float and sink.
☐ I can sort and group objects.
☐ I can record observations in a table.
☐ I can make predictions.

> 6.5 Magnets can pull

We are going to:
- investigate how magnets pull on magnetic materials
- make predictions about which materials are magnetic
- record observations in a table.

Getting started
- Have you seen any magnets?
- Tell a friend where you have seen magnets.

There are lots of different types of **magnets**.

Some materials are **magnetic**. They are pulled towards magnets.

Magnetic materials are pulled towards magnets by a magnetic force.

We say that they are **attracted** to magnets.

Materials that are not attracted to magnets are called **non-magnetic** materials.

Anita has lots of different types of magnets. Her magnet is pulling metal paper clips.

attracted   magnetic
magnet   non-magnetic

6 Forces

Think like a scientist

Which materials are magnetic?

> **You will need:**
> a magnet, some materials to test

Arun and Marcus use a magnet to test materials.

The magnetic materials are attracted to the magnets.

The magnets are not attracted to non-magnetic materials.

Arun tests a plastic chair

Arun tests a wooden ruler; Marcus tests metal

Arun records his results

Choose some materials to test.

Predict if they are magnetic.

Hold the magnet close to the material to see if it is magnetic.

Record your results in a table like the one on the next page.

6.5 Magnets can pull

Continued

Object	Material	Magnetic	Non-magnetic
door	wood		✓

Look at your results.

Try to see a pattern.

How am I doing?

Draw a magnet and three different objects which are attracted to it.

Do you have fridge magnets at home?

Sunil is testing his magnets.

They are attracted to the fridge door. Why?

They are not attracted to the wooden door. Why not?

135

6 Forces

Activity

Attracting metal paper clips

You will need:
a magnet, some materials to test

Shimna ties a metal paper clip onto a piece of string.

She holds the string with the paper clip at the end.

Predict what will happen as she moves the paper clip towards the magnet.

Tie a metal paper clip onto a string and test this yourself.

Draw what happened.

Would you like science lessons where you just look at pictures?
Do you like lessons where you do things? Why?

Look what I can do!

- ☐ I can investigate how magnets pull on magnetic materials.
- ☐ I can make predictions about which materials are magnetic.
- ☐ I can record observations in a table.
- ☐ I can say what happened and if my prediction was right.

Project

My things that move

Science helps you to understand how forces make things move.

You know the orange tug boats can pull the big ship.

Could the little red and white boat pull the big ship?

Find some things that move.

Find some pictures of things that move.

You could have:

- animals
- flying things
- games
- people
- toys
- balls
- things that slide
- things that roll.

6   Forces

Continued

Think about how these things move.

Talk about how they are pushed or pulled.

Talk about if they would float or sink.

Make a label to tell others about them, like this.

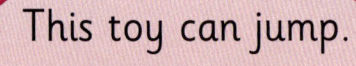

This toy can jump. We can push the handle. It would sink.

Check your progress

Talk about these questions.

1. Is the girl pulling or pushing?
2. How is the boy moving?
3. How are these people moving?

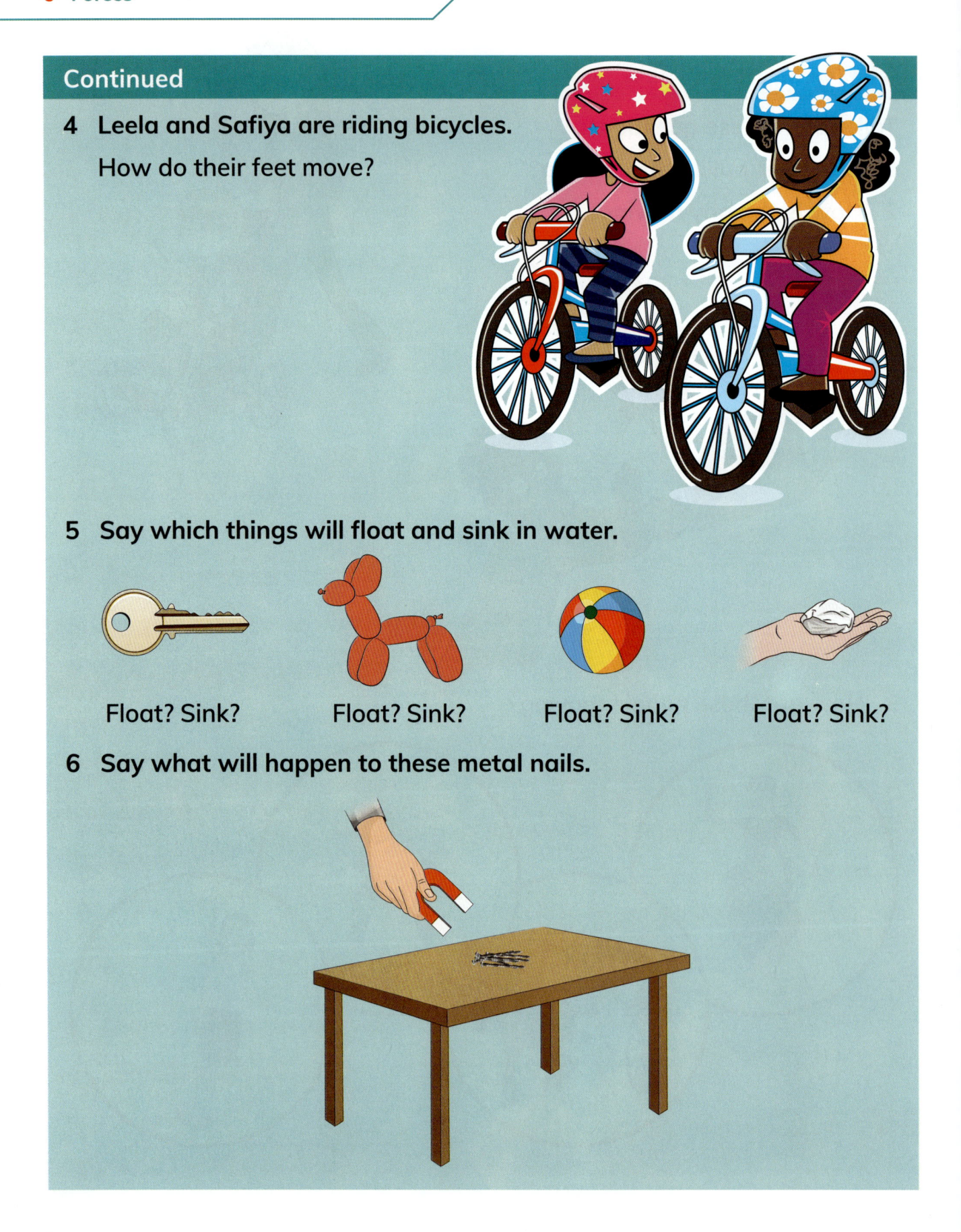

6 Forces

Continued

4 Leela and Safiya are riding bicycles.

How do their feet move?

5 Say which things will float and sink in water.

Float? Sink?   Float? Sink?   Float? Sink?   Float? Sink?

6 Say what will happen to these metal nails.

New science skills

Asking science questions

what?

how?

which?

why?

when?

There are many words you can use to ask a question.

Science questions often start with what, which, why, when or how.

What science questions do you have?

New science skills

How to use a magnifying glass

Hold the magnifying glass close to the object you are observing.

Move the magnifying glass slowly up and down, until you can see clearly.

How to find things out in science

1. Think of a question

Sofia and Arun have planted different seeds.
Sofia has a question.

Which plant will grow the fastest?

New science skills

2. Think about what will happen

Arun says what he thinks will happen.

I think they will all grow fast.

3. Talk about what to do to find the answer

Sofia and Arun will let the plants grow then look to see how tall they are.

4. Look carefully to find out the answer

This is called observing.

143

New science skills

Sometimes you can measure to find the answer

Sofia and Arun use bricks to measure how tall the plants are.

They write their results in a table.

Plant A	7
Plant B	5
Plant C	4

5. Talk about what you find out

Sofia and Arun found out that plant A grew the fastest.

They also found out that some plants grow faster than other plants.

Plant A grew the fastest.

I was not right. Some plants grow faster than others.

Glossary

air	the material that is all around us that we breathe to stay alive	101
alive	something that is living	3
animal	a living thing that eats other living things	3
answer	what you try to find out when you ask a question	10
ask	use a question to find out	10
astronaut	a person who travels in outer space	63
attract/ attracted	pull towards something	134
bend	change the shape of an object so it becomes curved, folded and not straight	54
blonde	hair that is yellow	98
body	the whole part of a human or other animal	89
breathe	to take in air using your mouth and nose	101
cell	a source of energy or power for a circuit	125
change	become different	34
compare	look at two or more things to find out how they are similar or different	33
compress	change the shape of an object by pushing or crushing it	54
damage	something is broken or hurt	27
danger	something that can cause us harm, for example, very loud sounds	29

die	stop living	70
different	something that is not the same	7
dry	not wet	77
dull	does not look bright when light shines on it, not shiny	44
ears	our organs with which we hear things	21
Earth	the planet that we live on	49
earthworms	long, thin, often red or brown animals that live in and make the soil	81
elastic	something that goes back into shape after being stretched, compressed, twisted or bent; a material that can stretch and return to its first shape	55
electricity	a form of energy	21
explain	when we give a reason for something	15
fabric	a soft, flexible material used to make clothes	42
far away	a long distance away (not near)	34
feel	use the sense of touch to find out	43
flexible	when something can bend easily	44
float	when an object stays at the surface of water, for example, an inflated rubber balloon	128
flower	part of a plant which makes fruit and seeds	6
force	a push or pull on an object	110
freeze	when very cold water turns to ice	70
gills	fish have gills that can take in air from water	101
glass	a material that is clear, used in windows	42
globe	a ball-shaped model of a planet or moon	71

group	to put things with other things that are similar in some way	4
grow	get bigger or change as you get older	9
hard	not easy to compress, not soft	44
healthy	something that is good for our bodies	101
hear	you hear sounds using your ears	21
hearing	you use your ears to hear sounds	92
heat	makes us warm	67
human	men, women and children are humans	89
instrument	something we use to make music	27
investigation	testing something to find the answer to a question	10
jump	move so that you are not touching the ground for a short time	112
label	a word written on a picture to name something in the picture	89
lake	a very large pool of water	61
land	the rocks and soils on the Earth's surface	62
leaf	part of a plant which makes food	6
light	a bright glow from a light source that helps us to see and enables plants to make food	10
list	a note of things we want to remember	23
listen	when we use our ears to hear sound	29
little	small	122
living	living things grow, need food, make waste, use air and reproduce	3

long	when two ends of something are far apart	90
look	to use your eyes to find things out	3
loud	a big sound	26
louder	more sound	27
machine	a mechanical device	115
magnet	a material, often metal, that is magnetic	133
magnetic	a material including some metals, which is attracted to magnets	133
magnifying glass	a magnifying glass makes things look larger so they are easier to see	7
mains	powerful electricity we use in buildings	125
materials	we use materials like wood, metal, plastic or glass to make many things that we use	42
metal	a material that is often strong and shiny	42
measure	find out how big a quantity is	56
model	a way we show how something works by making a small copy of something or a drawn example	6
Moon	a very large rocky object which travels around (orbits) a planet; the Moon orbits the Earth	64
move	change place or position	33
music	tunes played on instrument, sometimes with singing	27
name	the word we use for something	7
near	a short distance away (not far away)	34
non-living	something that is not alive	3
non-magnetic	a material which is not attracted to magnets, for example, wood, water	133
observe	using our senses to find out what is around us	6

paper	a material that you use to write on	42
parts	pieces of a bigger thing	5
pattern	an arrangement which we recognise, it might be repeated	81
planet	a ball of rock or gas in space which orbits the Sun	49
plant	a living thing that can make its own food	3
plastic	a man-made material that can be set into almost any shape	42
practical	a 'hands on' activity	15
predict	when we say what we think will happen	13
property	what something is like, for example a mirror is smooth and shiny	44
pull	try to draw towards you	110
push	pressing something	111
quarry	a place to dig up rock	74
question	you ask a question to find something out	10
quiet	less sound	26
record	when we draw or write a note of something we have observed	14
recycle	to make a used material into a new material	49
results	what we found out	24
rigid	when something cannot bend easily, not flexible	44
rock	a hard material found in the Earth, a very hard part of the Earth's surface	42
rolling	turning over and over	112
root	the part of a plant that grows down into the soil	6
rope	material twisted into a long cord	109

rough	bumpy, not smooth	46
rubber	a material that is very flexible and waterproof, used to make balloons	42
run	to move quickly	112
safe	not dangerous	21
same	similar in every way	98
science report	information given by a scientist	64
scientist	a person who does science	24
sea	large area of salty water	61
seeds	what plants grow from	5
senses	the things animals, including humans, use to find out about the world around them, how we know what is happening with sounds, sights, touch, taste and smells	27
shape	the outline of an object, e.g. square, cube, curved	53
shiny	looks bright when light shines on it	44
short	when two end of something are close together	90
sight	you use your eyes to see things	92
similar	being the same in some way	7
sink	when an object does not float, for example a metal key	128
skin	the material that covers our bodies	89
slide	move across a surface in contact with it	118
slope	a surface which starts high and ends low	112
smell	you use your nose to smell	92
smooth	not bumpy	46
soft	gentle to touch, not hard	44

soil	a mix of small pieces of rock, living things and living things that have died; plants grow in soil	78
sort	to put things into groups	46
sound	something you hear	21
source	a place where something starts	21
space	everything that is outside planet Earth	63
star	a light in the night sky, very big but very far away so it looks small	66
start	begin to move	117
stem	leaves and flowers grow from the plant stem	6
stop	end movement	117
stretch	change the shape of an object by pulling, making it longer or wider	55
strong	powerful, not easily broken	44
Sun	our nearest star which gives us heat and light	64
sunlight	light from the Sun	69
surface	the outside of something	62
swing	to move backwards and forwards	112
table	a grid where we record things	14
tall	how far it is from the bottom of something to the top	91
taste	you use your mouth to taste things	92
testing	doing something to find out what happens	51
threads	thin pieces of fabric that make up the material	46
tiny	very small	122
touch	you use your skin to feel things	92
turn	move to the right or left	112

twins	two children born at the same time to the same mother	98
twist	change the shape of an object by turning parts of it in different ways	54
unhealthy	something that is not good for our bodies	101
waste	when something is thrown away	49
water	a liquid substance that exists in seas, rivers and lakes which, when it is treated, we can drink	3
weak	not strong, easily broken	44
wet	covered in water	77
wood	a material that comes from the trunk of a tree	42

Acknowledgements

The authors and publishers acknowledge the following sources of copyright material and are grateful for the permissions granted. While every effort has been made, it has not always been possible to identify the sources of all the material used, or to trace all copyright holders. If any omissions are brought to our notice, we will be happy to include the appropriate acknowledgements on reprinting.

Thanks to the following for permission to reproduce images:

Cover illustration by Omar Aranda (Beehive Illustration); Inside *Unit 1* Wootthisak Nirongboot/GI; Leren Lu/GI; Dawid Kalisinski/EyeEm/GI; Jacky Parker Photography/GI; Chris Winsor/GI; phototropic/GI; NikkiZalewski/GI; Tuomas Lehtinen/GI; Alptraum/GI; Emilija Manevska/GI; Carol Yepes/GI; Michele D'Amico supersky77/GI; Davidhills/GI; *Unit 2* fotog/GI; Hill Street Studios/GI; Commerceandculturestock/GI; Les Imgrund/GI; Kool99/GI; alexandre17/GI; thegoodphoto/GI; Valentinarr/GI; Life On White/GI; Andy_Q/GI; Tambako the Jaguar/GI; G.Mazzarini/GI; Glyn Kirk/GI; Jose Luis Pelaez Stone/GI; SolStock/GI; Image Source/GI; *Unit 3* Halfdark/GI; Zocha_K/GI; MirageC/GI; Jay's photo/GI; Wladimir Bulgar/Science Photo Library/GI; Jimmyjamesbond/GI; Jacobs Stock Photography Ltd/GI; Rawpixel/GI; Steve Bronstein/GI; stockcam/GI; vitapix/GI; Fred Marie/Art in All of Us/Corbis/GI; JaggedPixels/GI; Enviromantic/GI; Ondacaracola photography/GI; PhanuwatNandee/GI; Rotofrank/GI; Sunstock/GI; FangXiaNuo/GI; photoka/GI *Unit 4* Tuul & Bruno Morandi/GI; Elena Duvernay/GI; Inhauscreative/GI; Nora Carol Photography/GI; Coolbiere Photograph/GI; Jose Luis Pelaez Inc/GI; AmyKerk/GI; Marco Guidi/GI; Jasius/GI; FokinOl/GI; Dimitri Otis/GI; VvoeVale/GI; Getty Images; Tim Grist Photography/GI; Prusak/GI; Deimagine/GI; Westend61/GI; Jeff Bottari/GI; David Malan/GI; Mik122/GI; thmacx/GI; Steve Allen/GI; Stefano Bianchetti/Corbis via Getty ImagesI; Stocktrek/GI; *Unit 5* WeAre/GI; Trevor Williams/GI; Rawpixel/GI; Cultura Exclusive/Ken Kiefer 2/GI; Lew Robertson/GI; marilyna/GI; XiXinXing/GI; *Unit 6* Dimitri Otis/GI; Paul J.Richards/GI; NASA/Roger Ressmeyer/VCG/GI; Solovyova/GI; Daniel Hurst Photography/GI; David Aaron Troy/GI; Ssj414/GI; fstop123/GI; Stefanie Wenk/EyeEm/GI; Daniel Milchev/GI; RinoCdZ/GI; Tcsaba/GI; Creative Crop/GI; Afi Hermatova/GI; Deepblue4you/GI; Kathryn8/GI; Ursula Alter/GI; Creative Crop/GI; Epsilon5th/GI; ruisergio/GI; Kruwt/GI; mcwhitey/GI; MariannaSaska/GI; olm26250/GI

GI = Getty Images